Everything — is gonna be all right

"*Everything Is Gonna Be All Right* is the portable Rev. Hasley—a welcome companion and friend—enjoyable to be with, inspiring to know, and yet challenging when necessary, though always with grace and humor. I have read many devotional books, but none quite so heartfelt, warm, and relatable. It is a gift."

—**Craig C. Hill,** Dean, Perkins School of Theology/SMU

"Robert Hasley's charming style and uplifting stories remind us of God's abiding presence amid challenging times and offer practical everyday hope. A joyful, accessible read guaranteed to inspire and renew your faith."

—**Dr. Jan Davis,** Senior Pastor, Central UMC, Fayetteville, Arkansas

"Robert's intimate stories throughout this devotional remind me to not lose sight of God's daily gifts in the midst of life's pains."

—**Mike Slaughter,** Pastor Emeritus Ginghamsburg Church,
Founder Passionate Churches, LLC.

"I was both moved and deeply enriched in my own Christian walk by Dr. Hasley's heartfelt sharing of his personal and entertaining life experiences. Your spiritual life will be enriched by the faith and encouragement expressed so beautifully in each devotional reading."

—**Jim Scoggin,** CEO, Methodist Health System Dallas

"At a time when so little seems to be "all right," Pastor Robert Hasley imparts wisdom inherited from his 101-year-old grandmother in faith-restorative devotionals. Hasley uncovers expressions of God's healing hand in events of everyday life."

—**Tim Cowlishaw,** columnist, Dallas Morning News

"These devotionals provide the assurance and peace that Robert's grandmother once gave him and that he now bestows upon us: 'Everything is gonna be all right!'"

—**Rev. Paul Rasmussen,** Highland Park UMC, Dallas, Texas

"Robert Hasley is a great friend. This book is a journey into his heart, and your heart will be warmed by reading it."

—**Rev. Edlen Cowley,** Senior Pastor, Fellowship UMC,
Trophy Club, Texas

Everything is gonna be all right

Devotionals for Faith and Encouragement

Robert Hasley

Plano, Texas

Everything Is Gonna Be All Right

This book is printed on acid-free, elemental chlorine-free paper.
ISBN 978-1-953495-01-3

20 21 22 23 24 25 26 27 28 29 —10 9 8 7 6 5 4 3 2 1
MANUFACTURED IN THE UNITED STATES OF AMERICA

In celebration of the 35th anniversary
of the St. Andrew faith family

&

In loving memory of
my grandmother, Maude Bryan Stephens
my parents, Carlton and Jeanne Hasley
my wife, Sharon's parents, Bill and Dorothy Collier
and my mentor and friend, Dr. Leighton K. Farrell

&

In honor of my wonderful wife, Sharon, our family,
the church family, and of my incredibly gifted partner
in ministry for over 25 years, Reverend Charles Stokes

The stories in this book arise from actual life
events involving family members,
friends, and acquaintances. My prayer is that
these ordinary life experiences will
help us clearly see that divine grace is perpetually
at work to remind us that, no matter
what, we are not alone in this life, and therefore
everything is truly going to be all right.

Everything — is gonna be all right

Acknowledgments

I want to offer my tremendous gratitude for the vision of Reverend Arthur Jones and Dr. Len Wilson which has led to the creation of a St. Andrew-affiliated publishing company called Invite Resources. The mission of Invite Resources is to share the promise of the New Creation by inviting people to discover a deeper faith and relationship with Christ, to use their gifts for the benefit of others, and to participate in God's kingdom. As such, it is a ministry designed for both lay and professional church leaders. Invite Press is a division of Invite Resources and is the publisher of this book. Many more books are to come. To learn more, visit inviteresources.com.

In addition, I want to offer a special thank you to the exceptional work of the team that edited and produced this work, including Diana McKnight, Kay Hutchens, Kay Richardson, Sharon Hasley, Barbara Bailey, Barbara Dick, Stephen Graham-Ching, and Len Wilson.

Robert Hasley
Plano, Texas
September 2020

Foreword

Andrew is sometimes described as the first evangelist. Scripture says that he brought his brother Peter to Jesus as well as others who wanted to know more about Jesus and the power of his faith in God. When over five thousand people gathered to hear Jesus speak and experience his presence, Andrew was the disciple who introduced Jesus to the boy who had with him the fishes and loaves that would be blessed to feed the hungry crowd. After Jesus took the five loaves and two fish, "… he looked up to heaven, and blessed and broke the loaves, and gave them to the disciples, and the disciples gave them to the crowds. And all ate and were filled; and they took up what was left over of the broken pieces, twelve baskets full. And those who ate were about five thousand men, besides women and children" (Matthew 14:19-21 NRSV). According to the Gospel of Matthew, Jesus fed not only five thousand men, but also the women and children who were there. No one went away hungry. All those who were fed had a firsthand experience of the power of Jesus and his faith.

In much the same way, those at St. Andrew United Methodist Church together affirm that "our faith in Christ is real, practical, and life changing." In 1985 what would become St. Andrew was a hope, a prayer, and a vision for a large piece of undeveloped land on what was then the very northern edge of west Plano, Texas. "[F]or in perfect faithfulness you have done marvelous things, things planned long ago" (Isaiah 25:1 NIV).

Of those chosen by God and called into ministry, some excel as preachers, others as teachers, others as counselors, and still others as pastors. For over thirty-five years, Rev. Robert Hasley has been the pastor to generations of those who worship at St. Andrew. Robert was appointed "for just such a time as this" (Esther 4:14 NRSV) to form a congregation and start a new church on a vacant site. From the beginning, Robert was prepared to "walk by faith, not by sight" (2 Corinthians 5:7 NRSV) into an unknown future and build what would become St. Andrew. As a true shepherd, Robert has blessed those at St. Andrew with the gift of his comfort, guidance, and direction.

Above all else, Robert is present to each individual entrusted to his care. In shepherding the St. Andrew family of faith, he has shared in the rites and rituals of both heartache and celebration through every circumstance of life. Robert leads from a heart that overflows with love, joy, and tender compassion for each member of his flock after the example of Jesus, the Good Shepherd, who said, "Feed my sheep" (John 21:17 NRSV). In this book of devotionals for faith and encouragement, Robert shares from this same heart some of the life experiences of love, loss, sorrow, and joy that have shaped his life and formed his faith. Over the years, he has used the lessons learned from his large and loving family to grow and cultivate the faith family of St. Andrew. In each heartfelt devotional Robert expresses the exponential power of faith to change our hearts and enrich our lives through the sufficiency of God's grace.

My late husband, Dr. Leighton Farrell, considered it one of the great blessings of his fifty years in ministry to be asked by Robert, whom he mentored in ministry, to join the staff of St. Andrew in 2000. It was a joy for him to be able to support Robert, to participate in the growth of the congregation, and to oversee the expansion of the physical facilities, including the construction of a new Sanctuary. On the last occasion that Leighton was in the pulpit at St. Andrew a few weeks before his untimely death, he offered this pastoral prayer: "We have come this far by faith and we will continue to walk with our hand in yours wherever you lead us."

I pray that your heart and soul will be blessed by the words of faith and encouragement in this devotional book, written in celebration of the thirty-fifth anniversary of the St. Andrew faith family. May you continue to worship, connect, serve, and give in the name of Jesus Christ, "And this is the victory that conquers the world, our faith" (1 John 5:4 NRSV).

Julie Yarbrough
Dallas, Texas
September 2020

Introduction

"Everything is gonna be all right."

While growing up in small towns in Arkansas—including the Springhill Community near Hope, Emmet, Mena, Van Buren, and Magnolia—I frequently heard my Grandmother Stephens say, "Everything is gonna be all right." She offered up these words of assurance when I skinned my knee or performed badly on a test, and later when I dropped a pass in a big game. These were comforting words, but I stopped believing them when I left home for Hendrix College in Conway, Arkansas.

At Hendrix, I saw friends go off to Vietnam and not return. I observed race riots. I watched Watergate unfold on television. I thought to myself, everything, in fact, may not be all right. Of course, I loved my grandmother and didn't want to hurt her, so I would make excuses for her, in my mind and occasionally to others. I'd say, well, you have to understand, she grew up in rural Arkansas. She was sheltered. She had a Pollyanna-like faith. Finally, I asked her, "How can you believe that everything is gonna be all right?" And when I listened, I heard for the first time about a remarkable life.

Grandmother Stephens was born in 1899 in a small lumber town in south Arkansas. She married at the age of eighteen. People married young in those days, but usually not that young. Her beau, Vernon, joined the U.S. Army to fight in the Great War, so they got married before he left home to serve his country.

Grandmother lived in fear that something would happen to him. Vernon survived and returned home to Gurdon, Arkansas, in late 1918, but an estimated nine million other soldiers did not return (*Encyclopedia Britannica*). Some of those were friends of my grandparents. After the war, Vernon and my grandmother made regular trips to the cemetery to visit friends and decorate headstones.

The next year, the Spanish Flu pandemic began. My grandparents survived, but between seventeen and fifty million people around the globe did not (*Washington Post*). Again, they visited friends in the cemetery and decorated headstones.

A decade later, the American economy crashed. Just when many young couples were getting on their feet, raising children, establishing a home, and reaching for financial milestones, the bottom fell out for my grandmother and grandfather. Where they lived in Gurdon, Arkansas was powered by the timber industry, which suffered greatly. My grandparents started saving every little thing they had. On more than one occasion, I saw my grandmother wash, dry, and fold a piece of aluminum foil and place it in a kitchen drawer to be reused. For the rest of their lives, they valued everything they had, because they knew the pain of having nothing. They survived the Great Depression, but many others did not.

When Grandmother turned 40, another global conflict erupted. Her son Robert enlisted to fight in World

War II. He became a naval aviator and served in the South Pacific. Three years later, he returned home, but between seventy-five and eight-five million soldiers and civilians died (*Oxford Companion to World War II*). Again, my grandparents went to the cemetery to visit friends and to decorate headstones.

Grandmother Stephens did not live a Pollyanna life; nor did she, as a life-long Methodist, have a Pollyanna faith. Her husband and my grandfather, Vernon, died at age seventy-five. For the next twenty-six years, Grandmother lived alone. During those years, she also attended the funerals of three of her four children: Ann, Bryan, and my mother, Jeanne. Grandmother experienced tremendous heartbreak and pain. Yet, despite all her grief, even into her old age, she would still say to me and to those around her, "Everything is gonna be all right."

In the meantime, I answered the call to become a pastor. I studied about Jesus and his followers in seminary. Jesus introduced his disciples to what it meant to trust in God, to have faith. At first, the disciples did not have faith, so they borrowed Jesus' faith, much like I borrowed the faith of my grandmother. However, a day came when the disciples saw their teacher arrested, crucified, and buried. At that moment, they questioned everything they had been taught about faith.

However, after all the heartache and disappointment, the Risen Jesus showed up in the middle of a locked room, showed the disciples his scars, and gave them peace. Jesus spent time with them, and, in that time, the disciples came to own their faith in a way they never had before. This was the foundational time for the church that was to come. Even then, one of the twelve disciples still struggled to trust. Like the others, Thomas had retreated in fear and doubt after Jesus was crucified. When Jesus appeared, Thomas said he wouldn't believe until he could touch the scars.

I can relate to Thomas. It has been said that all of us go through stages of faith development. First, we borrow our faith from parents, grandparents, prophets, pastors, and others who come before us. At some point, because of life's vagaries, we question that which we have borrowed. For some, that moment is college when we ask tough questions, and we either reject faith altogether or slowly begin to build our faith. In the midst of our struggles, God's grace can lead us to discover and embrace our own faith.

Grandmother Maude Stephens lived her life according to her faith. When I went off to college, however, I was like Thomas. I was no longer content to borrow faith from my grandmother. I needed to touch and feel faith for myself; my search led, not only to my own faith, but also to the pastorate to help others find faith.

My grandmother's life spanned three centuries. She lived to be 101 years of age. Not long before her passing, I visited Grandmother in the nursing home. Her eyesight had become so poor that the nurses had taken away the television and removed the pictures on the wall. Her room was bare except for her Bible and a Rolodex of family photos on a nightstand next to her bed.

For Grandmother, having God in her life along with the people she loved was sufficient. With these two sets of relationships as a present and future hope, she knew everything was gonna be all right.

Almost twenty years after my last visit with my grandmother, a friend stopped by my office to share how tough the COVID-19 pandemic had been for her. She was not allowed into the nursing home to visit her mother, so she had resigned herself to standing outside her mother's bedroom window and waving while talking to her on a cell phone. I listened as my friend shared her disappointment and frustration. Then I prayed with my friend and heard myself say to her just before she left my office that, by God's grace, everything is gonna be all right.

The stages of faith development—borrowed faith, seeking faith, and owned faith—are not linear. They are cyclical in nature as we move from one stage to another throughout our lives. Some days, we borrow our faith from others, and, in our questioning, we find faith in others and finally in ourselves.

Through these devotions, my prayer is that you will discover for yourself the true gift of a life of faith. In Psalm 23:4, David writes, "Even though I walk through the darkest valley, / I fear no evil; / for you are with me; / your rod and your staff— / they comfort me." The word *through* is significant. It means that, for every valley in life, there is both an entrance and an exit. Storms do not last. We will enter storms, but we will also exit them. That word *through* simply means, everything is gonna be all right.

Grandmother Stephens passed from this life to the next in the year 2000, at age 101, in a hospital in Gurdon, Arkansas. Her great-nephew sat at her bedside and sang the doxology at the moment she took the hand of the Lord and was led to God's heavenly kingdom. As he began to sing, the nurse joined, and then a patient across the hall, until the hallway was filled with this song of praise:

"Praise God, from whom all blessings flow;
Praise [God], all creatures here below;
Praise [God] above, ye heavenly host;
Praise Father, Son, and Holy Ghost. Amen."

Thomas Ken, 1674

Through every season of life—even in the midst of death—God is with us. With those we love around us, and us around them, everything is truly gonna be all right.

Yours in Christ,
Robert Hasley
Pastor | June 2020

Morning News
Key papers
missing in

Judge not

"Do not judge by appearances."

John 7:24

The annual Hasley reunion is a whirlwind affair. Once a year, we gather just outside of Arkadelphia, Arkansas. Our family gathering is very loud: first, due to the size of the crowd (my dad was one of twelve siblings); and second, because the Hasleys are known as "loud talkers." If you are shy or soft spoken, chances are you will not be noticed at a Hasley reunion.

For fifty years, one of my relatives by marriage has been attending the Hasley reunion. I had sized up this reserved man as someone who was not a significant player as far as family dynamics were concerned. But I was wrong! Visiting with him recently I learned the following: First, he and my father were very close. My parents loved and respected him. Second, he helped my father through a rough time, literally giving him the shirt off his back. Finally, he served in World War II from 1942 to 1944 in the Army Air Corp, flying fighters in the South Pacific. He was an authentic war hero! Previously unknown to me, this unassuming man had a significant impact on my faith and my family, and, because of his service and others like him, we have the freedom to congregate as a family today.

Just as we are taught not to judge a book by its cover, the same is true for people. This is a biblical principle. "Do not judge by appearances," says Jesus (John 7:24). Then Jesus declares, "Do not judge, so that you may not be judged.... Why do you see the speck in your neighbor's eye, but do not notice the log in your own eye?" (Matthew 7:1-3).

Simply put, we pay a price for judging others. I have rediscovered that I need to judge less and seek to understand more. I need to tone down my rhetoric and spend a lot more time listening to those around me. The greatest gift in life is the gift of relationship with God and others. So judge not and be blessed by wondrous new relationships with God's people.

Sit down and visit

“Jesus said, ‘Make the people sit down.’”

John 6:10

One of my favorite memories of my son John’s childhood happened when he was around age two. Often, when I came home from work, he would be sitting on the floor of our living room, den, or bedroom, playing with his toys. When I entered the room, he would stop what he was doing, look up at me, smile, pat the floor beside him, and say, “Sit down and visit.” I would gladly sit down. Sometimes he would talk and talk about random things, and I would just listen. Other times we would simply play together with his toys. We would not talk much, but we would make awesome sound effects of trucks crashing into each other or action figures in mortal combat. The bond of love between my son and me grew stronger each time I accepted John’s invitation to “sit down and visit.” I will always cherish those moments.

The apostle Paul reminds us that God extends to us an invitation to “sit down and visit”. Sometimes this invitation directs us to sit in a Chapel pew, on a park bench, or in a chair in a quiet room at home. Sometimes the occasion calls for us to sit and listen. On other occasions, there is a lot of conversation. But most importantly, Paul reminds us with words like "pray without ceasing" (1 Thess 5:17) and "persevere in prayer" (Rom 12:12) that we must not pass up the invitation to sit down and visit with God. We will come to find we cherish these special moments above all others; the bond of love between the Lord and us will grow stronger and stronger each time we say yes to the Lord's invitation. So join me in making it a priority this week to "sit down and visit" with God at least once each day. You and I will be glad we did.

I'm fixin' to

"And immediately they left their nets and followed him."

Mark 1:18

In the Hasley family, "I'm fixin' to" is a common response to requests to do chores around the house. Over the years, our children have made extensive use of this phrase. For them, "I'm fixin' to" meant either (1) I have more important things to do right now, so I'll get around to it later; or (2) I really don't want to do what I've been asked, and if I put it off long enough, maybe someone else will do it for me. Needless to say, I am not a fan of the phrase "I'm fixin' to."

When God asked Moses to lead God's people across the Red Sea to freedom, Moses didn't answer, "I'm fixin' to." After a brief protest, he did what God asked (see Exod 3:1–14:31). Jesus saw Simon and his brother Andrew casting a net into the sea and said to them, "Follow me and I will make you fish for people" (Mark 1:17). Simon and Andrew did not respond by saying, "I'm fixin' to." Instead, "immediately they left their nets and followed him" (v. 18). Instead of being "I'm fixin' to" people, Moses, Simon, and Andrew did what God asked them to do.

Before I come off sounding self-righteous, however, I have been known to use the phrase "I'm fixin' to" from time to time. My wife, Sharon, will attest to the fact that cleaning out the garage has been a perpetual "I'm fixin' to" project. As I look at my spiritual life, too many times I've responded to God's call to serve with the words, "I'm fixin' to."

Where do you need to make a change from "I'm fixin' to" to "I'm doing it"? We cannot make the change alone. Only by the power of God's redeeming grace through faith can we be transformed into people who are not "fixin' to" but "doing" what God asks of us. Will you say yes this very moment to follow God and become an instrument of love, joy, and hope in this world?

My faith is not circumstantial

"For I am convinced that neither death, nor life, nor angels, nor rulers, nor things present, nor things to come, nor powers, nor height, nor depth, nor anything else in all creation, will be able to separate us from the love of God in Christ Jesus our Lord."

Romans 8:38-39

"My faith is not circumstantial" is a direct quote from Dan Smith. Dan was a 40-year old member of our St. Andrew church staff who, as a result of a quickly-growing cancer, was placed on hospice care. Dan was a beloved and valued member of the St. Andrew family, serving faithfully on staff for nine years. During a visit to his home, he said to me that some friends had raised concerns about why, after so many prayers for healing, God had not cured his cancer. They wondered how he now must feel toward God.

Without hesitation, Dan declared, "My faith is not circumstantial." He indicated that he does not know why he has cancer. However, he does know that no set of circumstances would ever separate him from the love of God in

Christ Jesus his Lord (see Rom 8:38-39). Dan was crystal clear that his faith in God through Jesus Christ does not depend on the shifting circumstances of life. He believed that, just as God remains steadfast in God's love for him and his family, Dan had been called to remain strong and steadfast in his faith in the Lord God Almighty.

I was emotionally overcome by the power of Dan's personal testimony. Reverend Arthur Jones, who was also visiting with Dan, turned to me and said, "I have known Dan since I was four years old; he always lives what he believes." The way Dan had chosen to live his life serves as a phenomenal testimony today to what it means to be a passionate servant of Christ. Long after we all have physically departed this earth, I believe that Dan's heartfelt affirmation, "My faith is not circumstantial," will continue to echo through the ages as a powerful witness of unwavering faith in Jesus Christ.

May I have seconds?

"From his fullness we have all received,

grace upon grace."

John 1:16

While serving Holy Communion in Wesley Hall almost fifteen years ago, a 10-year-old boy asked a question that I had never been asked before and have not been asked since. Holding a plate with pieces of bread in one hand and a tray with small cups of juice in the other, I spoke to each congregant kneeling at the chancel rail: "This is the body of Christ broken for you and the blood of Christ shed for you." After serving the boy, I moved to serve the next person. However, before I could speak, the young man asked in a very loud whisper, "May I have seconds?"

Caught off guard by the question, I immediately began searching my mental files to determine if there was any theological principle or doctrinal statement that prevented me from giving this boy another piece of bread or cup of juice. I could not immediately come up with a reason not to serve him seconds.

I then began to think practically about the possible consequences of granting the young boy's request. Would answering yes begin a run of requests for seconds on the bread and juice, which we could not handle due to a shortage of supplies? Well, to make a long story short, I served seconds to the boy. His smile stretched from ear to ear as he ate another piece of bread and drank another cup of juice. His mom kept her head bowed the whole time, either because she was deep in prayer, laughing, or she didn't want to be recognized as his mom. Anyway, lightning didn't strike Mom, the boy, or me. In addition, there were no other requests for seconds that day or since.

Looking back on that eventful day, I believe that I was standing on solid biblical footing to serve seconds of Holy Communion to the young boy. John 1:16 reads, "From his [Jesus Christ's] fullness we have all received, grace upon grace." The definition of grace is unmerited favor. Whether the young boy knew it or not, by asking for seconds of the bread and juice he was symbolically asking for a second helping of God's grace. The correct answer as to whether or not we can receive a second helping of the grace of God is unequivocally and emphatically yes!

Could you use a second helping of God's unmerited love today? Have the courage to ask, as did the young boy, and you shall receive "grace upon grace."

The Lord's Body Shop

"Worship the Lord your God, / and serve only him."

Matthew 4:10

My family and I recently attended the annual Hasley reunion at DeGray Lake, just outside of Arkadelphia, Arkansas. Having learned that the road in front of the old Hasley farm in Gum Springs (a suburb of Arkadelphia) had been named Hasley Road, I took the family to see "our" road. I found the road but not a road sign or any evidence of the old Hasley farm. We did come across an old, broken-down shed with a sign that read "Hasley's Body Shop." My three sons, Stephen, John, and Will, saw this as an opportunity to pose for a photo with muscles flexed (since none of us have a clue about car repairs) in front of Hasley's Body Shop.

Over time, so much changes. It seems like yesterday that I was gathering eggs, playing touch football or riding horses with my cousins in the pasture next to the Hasley farmhouse. Now, only the broken-down "Hasley's Body Shop" sign remains. While life itself changes, the need to remember and connect with family does not. Making the connection helps me remember who I am and whose I am. The result of re-grounding is renewed direction and strength (muscles) to be all I was raised to be.

My hope is that my family and I will visit Hasley's Body Shop at least once each year. The Lord has a body shop, too; it is called the Sanctuary or worship center. And we are invited to visit every week. We go there to work on our spiritual muscles. We go to the "Lord's Body Shop" to reconnect with God and our faith family. When we leave, we have a better understanding of whose we are and who we are. In worship, we are repaired by the Lord so that we can face the challenges each day brings with clearer direction and renewed strength. Our worship prepares us to be all that God created us to be. So, remember to visit the "Lord's Body Shop" soon.

All the fixin's

"For God so loved the world that he gave his only Son, so that everyone who believes in him may not perish but may have eternal life."

John 3:16

I was serving as a summer youth director for a small United Methodist church in South Arkansas. The pastor was out of town one weekend, and I was left in charge of the Sunday morning worship service. At the conclusion of the service, I stepped forward and called for anyone who would like to join the family of faith to come forward. Someone did, and wanted to be baptized. I panicked, realizing that I had no authority as a non-ordained, 20-year old college student, to baptize anyone. So, I turned to the congregation and said, "When Brother Bill returns next Sunday, he will do all the fixin's." Laughter followed. Lots of laughter.

Not only is the word fixin's not in the Holy Bible, it is not found in any Christian literature that the members of that church family had ever read. In addition, fixin's, for those who grew up in the South, meant all those ancillary items that accompanied the main course of a dinner or supper. Now, the argument could be made—and was made by several members of that congregation—that baptism, or the public act of accepting Jesus Christ as your Lord and Savior, is the main course when it comes to faith. In no way or at no time should baptism be referred to as "all the fixin's."

There are times when we each need to be reminded of those things that are essential to living life meaningfully and abundantly and those things that are not necessary. It is relatively easy to be sidetracked from what is significant.

Stop in the name of love

"There is therefore now no condemnation for those who are in Christ Jesus."

Romans 8:1

The gift of parenthood was bestowed upon my sister, Barbara, and my brother-in-law, Jeff, with the birth of Callie in 2001. As in most families, they found that parenting a three-year-old is particularly challenging. One day, Barbara had reached the limit of her patience and surprised even herself when she shouted "Stop!" in response to Callie's behavior.

Barbara could clearly see that Callie was startled by her forceful response and was near tears. Then, in an all-out attempt to head off the meltdown, Barbara began dancing and singing "Stop! In the name of love, before you break my heart." Barbara even added hand motions to this classic song by the Supremes. The result? Callie not only did not cry but, in time, began singing and dancing herself. Her behavior changed (for the moment) and the bond of love between a mother and daughter grew stronger that day.

There are a lot of unwanted behaviors that God would like for us to stop, especially unhealthy behaviors that are destructive to ourselves and others. However, instead of shouting at us for our shortcomings, "God so loved the world that he gave his only Son… in order that the world (we) might be saved through him" (John 3:16-17).

Simply, rather than condemning us, God loved us into a relationship through the unconditional love and sacrifice of God's Son, Jesus Christ. The intended result is that we will stop our unloving ways because we do not want to break the heart of God who loves us; nor do we want to break the hearts of God's children. So, pray with me this week that we can stop condemning and judging, and instead spend a lot more time singing, dancing, loving, and praising God and others!

The Rufous Hummingbird

"The one who had received the one talent went off and dug a hole in the ground and hid his master's money."

Matthew 25:18

By observing the behavior of birds and animals which God created, I believe that we can gain insight into our human condition. Recently, a beautiful orange, green, and white bird called the Rufous Hummingbird was for me a source of just such insight into human behavior. I had set up two bird feeders, twenty yards apart, outside a friend's cabin in Colorado. Immediately, five hummingbirds showed up to feast on enough sugar water to feed over one hundred hummingbirds. But surprisingly, the Rufous Hummingbird proceeded to claim both feeders as her territory. She positioned herself either on top of the feeders or on a nearby tree from which she could keep an eye on both feeders. Each time one of the other hummingbirds attempted to drink from a feeder, she flew at them, chasing them away from the nectar. She aggressively kept the other birds away not only that day but for the several days I was at the cabin. During that time, not once did she allow another bird to drink. Furthermore, she seldom drank from the feeders herself because she was too busy keeping the other birds away from what she clearly considered to be her property. The way I saw it, the Rufous Hummingbird was on her way to a lonely and malnourished existence if her behavior did not change.

Jesus talked about a man who was given one talent by his master. Because he was so worried and afraid of losing the gift, he hid it in the ground rather than investing it for growth or sharing it with others. So the gift was lost. The implication of the parable was that this man spent the remainder of his life malnourished relationally and spiritually (Matt 25:14-30). Our lives and possessions are gifts from God that are to be used to serve God by serving God's people.

The behavior of the Rufous Hummingbird, along with the parable of talents, reminds us that if we hoard the gifts we have been given, we will be malnourished—not necessarily physically, but certainly spiritually—and we will be alone. Instead of living out of fear, let's commit to living in faith. Let's stop hoarding our possessions, and instead use our God-given gifts of time, talents, and financial resources to serve God by serving others.

A thought on **reunions**

"And remember, I am with you always, to the end of the age."

Matthew 28:20

To be honest, I have not been a big fan of reunions. As a matter of fact, I have missed more than my share of reunions. In my opinion, there is far too much posturing, comparing, competing, and judging that takes place at these gatherings. At least, that is what I have told myself when I have declined or failed to respond to an invitation.

After my wife, Sharon, attended her high school reunion a few years back, I asked her why she went. She said, "I just want to know that my classmates are doing all right." Over the years, I have heard many reasons for attending reunions: it's a great party, to show off pictures of kids and grandkids, to reconnect with people we have not seen for some time, or just curiosity as to how the passage of time has changed people physically, emotionally, vocationally, and relationally. However, I do not remember ever hearing that someone's primary reason for going to a reunion was to check on people you care about to see that they are all right.

As I think about it, Jesus was a big fan of reunions. After his death and resurrection, he created opportunities to reunite with his followers in a garden outside a tomb, in the upper room, on the road to Emmaus, by the sea, and on a mountain. In the past, I thought of these appearances as simply additional opportunities for Jesus to impart directives as to the future work and mission of his disciples. Is it possible that a primary reason for these reunions was to check on his friends and followers to make sure they were all right? Could it be that he cared about them enough to find a way to reconnect with them? I believe that the answer is yes. While reunited with his disciples on a mountaintop outside Galilee, he offered these comforting words: "And remember, I am with you always, to the end of the age" (Matt 28:20). At this life-changing reunion, Jesus communicated clearly how much he valued his friends. His desire was that the relationship that he had with them would be everlasting.

So, instead of seeing reunions as something to avoid or dread, maybe reunions can become gifts to be celebrated. How would our perception of reunions change if we approached them as opportunities to let others know how much we value them and appreciate the relationships we have with them? How would our commitment to a weekly reunion we call worship change if this were our perspective? Our presence in worship would become for us an opportunity to express to God and others how much we value and care for them.

More than a game

"The greatest of these is love."

1 Corinthians 13:13

One Friday night, I was at the ballpark in Arlington, watching one of the most dramatic wins in the history of Texas Rangers baseball. Nellie Cruz hit a walk-off home run in the thirteenth inning to beat the New York Yankees. A new record was established when a combined nineteen pitchers were used in the game. Even with all the heroics and statistical records set that evening, what I cherished the most was that my son John and I were there together.

In time, I will forget the score, records, and heroes of the game (as I have most games I have ever attended), but I will not forget the joy of spending the evening with my son. We talked, laughed, cheered, groaned, gave high fives, and even hugged each other while celebrating big plays. In the middle of the action, I recalled a time, forty-eight years ago, when I sat with my father in Yankee Stadium, watching Mickey Mantle and Roger Maris play ball. I don't remember the score of that game, who pitched, or who got a hit, but I do remember my dad buying me a Yankee megaphone filled with popcorn. I still have the megaphone and, even more, I have the memory of a very special afternoon spent with my dad at the ballpark.

So today, if you ask me which is my favorite sport, I will tell you that it is baseball. Why? Because my most cherished memories of time spent with my dad revolve around the baseball games we watched together. Now, my sons and I are creating those same memories. For me, baseball is far more than a game; it is about relationships with people I love.

In Ecclesiastes 3:1-8, we read:

> "For everything there is a season,
> and a time for every matter under heaven:
> a time to be born, and a time to die;
> a time to weep, and a time to laugh;
> a time to throw away stones,
> and a time to gather stones together;
> a time to embrace,
> and a time to refrain from embracing;
> a time to love, and a time to hate:
> a time for war, and a time for peace."

I would add, that, for me at least, there is also a time for baseball.

Wrestling with a kangaroo

"(God) wrestled with (Jacob) until daybreak."

Genesis 32:24b

I had taken my recent high school graduate, Will, with me on a study leave to Sydney, Australia, at Evangelist Alan Walker's College of Evangelism. During our free time, we saw some of the sites, including a zoo, which was highly recommended by the locals. We petted a koala, peered at a Tasmanian devil up close, and were ushered into a pen where we interacted with kangaroos. Will walked up to a juvenile kangaroo to feed it. Within a matter of seconds, the kangaroo's arms were wrapped around Will's neck in what appeared to be a wrestling hold. When we returned home to Plano, one of my top three stories from our trip was Will's unexpected wrestling match with a kangaroo.

Don't we all experience unanticipated wrestling matches along our life journey? We wrestle with family members, friends, bosses, choices we are about to make or have already made, uncertainty, loss, fear and even faith. The Old Testament character, Jacob, wrestled with the Lord God Almighty by the River Jabbok and the outcome of this struggle was a new faith and confidence in whose he was, who he was, and his God-given purpose on this earth. Both Jacob and the people of Israel were thankful for the wrestling hold that the Lord God put on Jacob which remained in place throughout his life.

Will was able to free himself from the kangaroo's headlock; however, the Lord God got a hold on him during college which has led Will to choose a life of service focused on building God's kingdom on earth as it is in heaven. Are you prepared to be blessed by going a round or two with the Lord today?

If the shoe doesn't fit, then what?

"The Spirit of the Lord is upon me, / because he has anointed me / to bring good news to the poor. / He has sent me to proclaim release to the captives / and recovery of sight to the blind, / to let the oppressed go free, / to proclaim the year of the Lord's favor."

Luke 4:18-19

You have heard the old saying, "If the shoe fits, wear it." Well, what if your shoe doesn't fit? The obvious answer is to throw away the old one and get a new pair of shoes. However, I suggest that is easier said than done. First, you have to know that the shoes you are wearing do not fit. Then, you must be willing to change out the old shoes for a new pair.

A few years ago, I went to the Cooper Aerobics Center for a physical. A part of the checkup included an examination of my feet to determine the make and model of tennis shoe that best fit my workout needs. I responded with shock and disbelief when I was informed by a fitness instructor that I had been wearing a tennis shoe a full size too small. I thought that they had to be mistaken. They either mixed up my foot measurement with someone else's, or they just measured my feet inaccurately. I wore a size ten in high school. I had worn a size ten shoe throughout my adult life. Furthermore, I would wear a size ten shoe until I died! No one was about to tell me something different! But the instructor explained that typically, as a person ages, the width and length of a person's foot will expand (as do other body parts). Therefore, the old shoe becomes too small. A larger shoe size is needed.

Almost two thousand years ago, Jesus came to say that the size of faith that most people were wearing was too small. This was especially the case for religious people, who believed that the Lord God was present to bless and redeem only the faithful few. Jesus tried to get them to throw away their old faith for a new and larger faith. He showed them the way when he proclaimed in the synagogue in Nazareth,

> "The Spirit of the Lord is upon me,
> because he has anointed me
> to bring good news to the poor.
> He has sent me to proclaim release to the captives
> and recovery of sight to the blind,
> to let the oppressed go free,
> to proclaim the year of the Lord's favor."
>
> Luke 4:18-19

However, people were shocked by the news that their faith was too small and fiercely protested any change to a larger faith.

I protested the recommendation to throw away my old shoes and buy larger ones. But then, I remembered the visit I had made to my doctor a year earlier, complaining about the pain and numbness I had been feeling in my toes. He found no medical reason for these symptoms. So I begrudgingly followed the trainer's advice and tried on a larger size shoe. The pain and numbness vanished. The comfort was phenomenal, and the spring returned to my step when I walked.

Is the faith you are wearing too small? If so, you might try on a larger size faith as taught and practiced by our spiritual trainer, Jesus of Nazareth. With the change, see if a spring returns to your step and a new joy fills your heart.

The whale that wasn't

"You shall love the Lord your God with all your heart, and with all your soul, and with all your mind.... You shall love your neighbor as yourself."

Matthew 22: 37-39

For a high school graduation present, I took my son Stephen to Alaska. This adventure was an opportunity for us to spend time together. I looked forward to hearing about his fears, hopes, and dreams as he entered his college years. The trip included a sightseeing cruise off the Kenai Peninsula. My heart was set on sighting a whale. To see a whale in the ocean would be a first for both of us. We boarded the boat and gathered with all the passengers on the top deck in anticipation of a sighting. Of course, after gathering, we were reminded by the captain that there was no guarantee that we would see a whale. Time passed. Then more time passed with no sightings. A few became discouraged and made their way down to the main cabin. I simply squinted harder, blocking out everyone and everything around me. I was determined to at least catch a glimpse of this monster of the sea.

Then, I could hardly believe my eyes. Suddenly, a long, black object appeared in the water. I yelled, "It's a whale!" Then, as if no one heard me the first time, I yelled again, “It’s a whale. There! See it! Isn’t it amazing?” As the crowd rushed over to where Stephen and I were standing to get a look at this creature from the deep, the captain’s voice came loudly and clearly over the intercom system, “Sir, that isn’t a whale, that’s a rock.” As I turned toward my son in disbelief, he had managed to move away from where we were standing, as if he didn’t know me. The rest of the passengers quickly moved to other parts of the boat.

The main reason for the Alaska trip was to get closer to my son. So it was ironic that, after this incident, we were standing far apart. How many times does our obsession with relatively insignificant personal agendas distract us from the important things in life, like being present for those who are most significant to us? The way I see it, Jesus came into our lives to teach us what is most important and how to keep that at the forefront. He said, “You shall love the Lord your God with all your heart, and with all your soul, and with all your mind,” and “You shall love your neighbor as yourself” (Matt 22:37, 39).

Simply, Jesus tells us that nothing is more significant than our relationships with God and each other. I do still enjoy whale watching. However, there are rocks and pitfalls we need to avoid. I believe that looking at the world through the lens of faith will help us to see more clearly the next time.

Givers and takers

"They are to do good, to be rich in good works, generous, and ready to share... so that they may take hold of the life that really is life."

1 Timothy 6:18-19

Two men in well-worn jeans and jackets were sitting in rusted folding chairs outside the gas station in Chidester, Arkansas. They were philosophizing on the meaning of life. As I walked by, I heard one of them declare, "There are only two kinds of people on earth: those who are givers and those who are takers." As a second-year graduate student, I thought the comment lacked sophistication and qualified as downright uneducated hogwash (Arkansan for that which is not based on factual data).

However, over the past thirty years, I have come to believe there was more wisdom in that homespun philosophy than I first believed. I especially notice this distinction as I sit with families as they plan a memorial service for a loved one. As I talk with the family about how they would like their loved one to be remembered, I have found that family members cannot say enough about individuals who have spent their lives giving of themselves to others. However, the conversations about those who have spent most of their lives taking from others are brief and without a great deal of substance. For me, the memorial services for those who have given little in their lifetime, but consumed a great deal, lack the elements of joy, peace, and celebration. I believe that joy, peace, and celebration are God-given gifts of a life well spent in service to God and others.

This week, I encourage you to reflect on Paul's words to Timothy to command the people of the faith community in Ephesus "to do good, to be rich in good works, generous, and ready to share… so that they may take hold of the life that really is life" (1 Tim 6:18-19). Some believe that there are only two kinds of people on earth. Which kind are you? When your life on earth comes to an end, how will you be remembered? Our hope resides in knowing that, by the grace of God through Jesus Christ, we can choose to live as we were created to live and to be remembered as "givers."

When it comes to faith, where do you stand?

"Then Mary said, 'Here am I, the servant of the Lord; let it be with me according to your word.'"

Luke 1:38

The last time I traveled to Magnolia, Arkansas, I took time to visit the cemetery where my parents are buried. As I stood next to the horizontal headstones marking the burial site, I became aware that I was standing between two vertical stone monuments that towered over this section of the cemetery. One monument had the words of the Lord's Prayer inscribed on it and the other had a painted image of the Last Supper. I thought this was an appropriate testimony to the faith of my parents. The Lord's Prayer is a reminder that our first priority is to love God by honoring and glorifying God's name in all that we say and do. My mom and dad honored God by joining the community of faith for worship every Sunday morning and evening. They led the way as financial supporters of the ministry of their church. Mom volunteered to teach Sunday school, sing in the church choir, and play the handbells. She was active in United Methodist Women and was elected president of her Sunday school class. Dad served on the Administrative Board, the Finance Committee, and the Staff Parish Relations Committee. Clearly, they chose to honor God by making the church central to their lives and to the lives of their children.

The painting of the Lord's Supper is a reminder of the sacrificial love of Christ. His body was broken and his blood was shed so that we might live abundant lives, free from sin. My father, as a public school superintendent, literally wore out his heart fulfilling his God-given calling to stamp out illiteracy. His mission was to provide the highest quality education possible to the students residing in his school district. As my mom faced the last days of her battle with cancer, she said to me, "Robert, I have fulfilled my God-given purpose, which was to give birth and parent you and your sisters. I am at peace." Both of my parents believed that Christ loved them so much that he was willing to make the ultimate sacrifice on their behalf. Likewise, because of their love for Christ, they were willing to make the sacrifices necessary to provide for the needs of others, including the needs of their children.

My reflections on my parents' deep and abiding faith have led me to ask what images might best define where I stand with my faith. What two monuments best define my discipleship? Two troubling images that crossed my mind were that of the Bethlehem innkeeper on one monument and an image of King Herod on the other. For me, the innkeeper symbolizes times when our lives are so preoccupied with small insignificant "stuff" that we have no room for Christ to reside in our lives. Herod characterizes the times we are tempted to spend our energy and resources serving only ourselves. My greatest desire is that my faith will reflect the characteristics of the faith of my parents. Their faith stands, alongside the faith of Mary and Joseph (see Matt 1:18-25), as my standard for what it means to put complete trust in God. Like the parents of a child born in a manger in Bethlehem, they dedicated their lives to seeking out and following the will of God, no matter the cost.

As you prepare to celebrate the difference the birth of Christ has made in your life, which two images best define the state of your faith? In other words, which images or inscriptions most accurately describe your relationship with God and others? The good news is, if you are not satisfied with the present condition of your faith, you can choose—with God's help—to change where you are now standing. You can reposition yourself to live out the rest of your days standing between the Lord's Supper and the Lord's Prayer. Your life can be a testimony of faith akin to that of Joseph and Mary. It's all about where you choose to stand, either at the center of God's selfless grace or at the center of worldly self-absorption. I am thankful for the saints who have gone before us, pointing the way to the solid ground of faith.

The cat in the Christmas tree

"To you is born this day in the city of David a Savior, who is the Messiah, the Lord."

Luke 2:11

One winter evening years ago, I was walking by our ornately decorated Christmas tree when it happened. With lightning speed, a paw with claws darted out from branches located halfway up the tree. Startled, I jumped back. Then, after gathering myself, I cautiously approached the scene of the attack. Midway up the tree, I spotted a patch of yellow among the branches. After drawing a little closer, I saw the culprit, crouching in his lair. It was our short-haired yellow tabby, Butterball. He was poised to attack the next victim who dared to venture too close to the brightly-lit tree.

For some time following this surprising incident, our family stayed a safe distance from our tree. However, as time passed, we would walk closer and closer to see if a yellow paw would reach out to grab us. It did, again and again. We actually began to look forward to being grabbed by the cat in our Christmas tree, and we delighted in having our friends experience the same.

Upon reflection, I believe there are some parallels that can be drawn to our approach to celebrating Christmas. God wants to reach out and grab our hearts and souls with the story of the birth of Jesus, God's Son and our Savior. Yet, more times than we might care to admit, we approach Christmas with caution. Maybe we are wary of being disappointed by what God has to offer, or we are afraid of the pain that might result from the claws of judgment. Whatever our reason, we often attempt to keep a safe distance between us and a personal relationship with the Christ child. But I also believe that a part of us wants to be grabbed by the true meaning of Christmas. We have a desire to walk close enough to the manger that Christ will be able to reach out his hand and touch us with his love, joy, and eternal hope. Then, we would like to give that same gift to our family and friends this Christmas.

My question to you is, why are you waiting? Walk a little closer to the manger this Christmas and let the love of Christ reach out and grab you.

When screaming is necessary

"Then [Jesus] entered the temple and began to drive out those who were selling things there; and he said, 'It is written, "My house shall be a house of prayer"; but you have made it a den of robbers.'"

Luke 19:45-46

It was a beautiful Sunday morning when my dad parked the car across the street from the First Methodist Church in Mena, Arkansas. My parents, my sister Sara, and I (we were both in elementary school at the time) waited at the intersection to cross the busy street between us and the front door of the Sanctuary. I didn't see a car coming, so I decided to step out and lead the way. From behind me came a piercing scream. I stopped and turned around to see that the person screaming was my sister. At that very instant, a car flew past within a foot of where I was standing. I had overheard my mom telling my sister that screaming was not ladylike, but I was thankful that she chose not to be a lady at that particular moment. Sara's scream probably saved my life.

There are times when screaming is not only appropriate but necessary. I believe that God screams from time to time. God screams in an attempt to stop people from hurting themselves or others. For example, Jesus screamed at the moneychangers in the temple for harming the poor and powerless through their money-making schemes (Luke 19:45-46). When Peter lost sight of God's purpose and mission, Jesus raised his voice to his own disciple, exclaiming, "Get behind me, Satan!… [Y]ou are setting your mind not on divine things but on human things" (Matt 16:23).

People can physically die if hit by a car; they can spiritually die by falling prey to sin (separation from God). Either case may call for a little yelling, hollering, and screaming from time to time to help them avoid death. As followers of Christ, we are called to be his voice of life in the world. Depending on the circumstance, the decibel level will vary.

It works better if you aim

"You did not choose me but I chose you. And I appointed you to go and bear fruit, fruit that will last."

John 15:16

The beautiful weather was beckoning a friend and me to go outside and play golf. After several holes, I stepped up on the green to putt. I missed, badly. My friend looked at my golf ball, then turned and looked up at me with a wry smile. He commented in a matter-of-fact tone, "It works better when you aim." I attempted to come up with a witty comeback but was unsuccessful. He had me. I had not read the curvature of the green or lined up my putt. I had not taken the time or made the effort to assume a comfortable putting stance. I had just stepped up to the ball and hit it in the general direction of the hole. That did not work so well. I did not get the desired result.

Since then, I have thought about the temptation that we all face to take a similar approach to the way we live our lives. All too often, we fail to take aim at a life goal or purpose. Instead, we aimlessly wander through life and observe less-than-desirable outcomes.

Jesus believed that life works better when you take aim. He approached life with a clear purpose given to him by God. That purpose is found in the following words from the Gospel of John: "For God so loved the world that he gave his only Son, so that everyone who believes in him may not perish, but may have eternal life. Indeed, God did not send the Son into the world to condemn the world, but in order that the world might be saved through him" (John 3:16-17). Jesus taught his followers that they, too, had a God-given purpose. All that was required of them was to align their lives with that purpose. In other words, they were to take aim at the mission that God placed in front of them.

It is a good time for all of us to focus and take aim at God's purpose for our lives. As followers of Christ, God has a purpose or mission for each of us. What is your mission? I believe that you will find that life works better if you take the time and effort to aim your life toward God's mission for you.

That's a lousy date

"Therefore encourage one another and build up each other."

1 Thessalonians 5:11

One day several years ago, Sharon and I drove to Flower Mound to visit my sister, brother-in-law, and niece. My niece Callie was nine years old at the time and called me Uncle Papaw. Since Callie has no living grandfather, she determined that I could fill two roles for her as both her uncle and grandfather. I was happy to oblige.

After a good visit, I said that it was about time for Sharon and me to leave for a date we had planned for that evening. Callie overheard the conversation and asked me, "Where are you taking Aunt Sharon for your date?"

I responded, "I'm taking her with me to a hospital in Fort Worth where I am visiting a patient who is a relative of a church member."

Callie looked at me strangely, and then with her index finger motioned me to come closer. As I bent down, she cupped her hand around her mouth and spoke softly but emphatically into my ear, "Uncle Papaw, that's a lousy date. You need to buy Aunt Sharon some flowers or something." Out of the mouth of a child can come amazing wisdom.

You know, over the years I have come to believe everyone needs a Callie in his or her life. We all need someone who knows us well enough and loves us enough to help and encourage us to be our best. The members of the family of faith, the church—at their best—are Callies to one another. They hold one another accountable to faithfully serve as messengers of the love of Christ to the world. We need feedback from others to help us remain aligned with our God-given purpose.

How many times this week, or this month, have you either listened to a Callie or been a Callie for someone else who needs a loving word of wisdom and guidance? The only way we will grow stronger in our personal faith or as a church family is to help one another stay on the path of Christian discipleship. The best way to accomplish this is to be a part of a small group in the church.

Who is your group of Callies? Who confronts you about lousy choices and celebrates with you when you make good decisions? If you do not meet with a small group, join or start one today. If you do not believe that you need help and encouragement on your journey of faith, become part of a fellowship group, covenant group, Bible study, or Sunday school class to help someone else stay on the path of faith. The apostle Paul reminds us that to remain strong as a family of faith it is essential to "encourage one another and build up each other" (1Thess 5:11).

He carried my bags

"If anyone strikes you on the right cheek,

turn the other also."

Matthew 5:39

Growing up, I not only loved my father, I idolized him. I spent a great deal of time and energy doing those things that would gain his respect and approval. Even my choice of a college was, in large part, an effort to make my dad proud. While in college, however, I began to mature and realize that I had to live my life based on my unique God-given gifts and God's calling and purpose for my life. I subsequently chose a new educational and vocational direction that was not aligned with my dad's vision for my future.

I completed my first year of college where I had initially enrolled. Then I flew home to enroll at a different college for the fall. The last thing I expected was that my father would pick me up at the airport. Over the telephone, we had exchanged some harsh words about my decision, which then turned into a cold, silent war of sorts. I looked for my mom as I walked off the airplane. To my great surprise, it was my father who was standing at the gate to welcome me home. He insisted that he carry my bags to the car.

I have learned a great deal about forgiveness over the

years. I have been taught that God calls upon us to turn the other cheek (Matt 5:39) and to forgive not seven times but "seventy times seven" (Matt 18:22 THE MESSAGE). However, I have never learned more about forgiveness (other than from the example of Jesus himself) than I learned that day from my dad at the airport. He put aside his pain, disappointment, and his pride. In welcoming me home, he clearly and emphatically let me know how much he loved me and that he forgave me. Then, he picked up my bags and carried them. With my dad by my side, I walked toward the new and uncertain future that, with God's help, I had chosen. As one who has received forgiveness, I pray when opportunities present themselves that I, too, will offer to carry the luggage of those I need to forgive. I am blessed beyond words to have had a bag carrier as a father. He was a true follower of the teachings of Jesus.

I can take him

"Whoever wishes to be great among you must be your servant."

Mark 10:43

My wife, Sharon, and I were walking around the track at Plano West Senior High when I spotted him. James Lofton, an NFL Hall of Fame wide receiver, had at one time played for the Green Bay Packers, the newly crowned Super Bowl champs. He was sitting on the track, putting on his running shoes for a workout. All I can say in my defense is that my brain was not functioning at full capacity when the following words came spewing out of my mouth: "I can take him." Of course, I was declaring that I could beat him in a foot race. James Lofton was a track star at Stanford, known for his blazing speed in the NFL. I, on the other hand, had once won the 100-yard dash in a track meet against Smackover High School. Sharon looked at me, then at James Lofton, who was in phenomenal physical condition. She looked back at me and said, "Yes, dear, you can take him as long as he remains in a sitting position." A squeeze of my hand and a kiss on my cheek followed.

Sometimes, we view life as a competition to be won rather than a God-given gift to be enjoyed in service to

God and others. Hindsight tells me that after spotting James Lofton, I might have said to Sharon, "I admire that man for all he has accomplished through a combination of hard work and good stewardship of his God-given gifts." I then could have celebrated and even complimented him for the grace and speed he exhibited as he ran around the track, rather than downplaying his strengths in an effort to highlight my own. Isn't that what James and John, the sons of Zebedee, attempted to do as they requested that they sit on Jesus' right and left in his glory, in lieu of other disciples occupying those seats? Jesus' reply to their request is worth repeating: "[W]hoever wishes to become great among you must be your servant; and whoever wishes to be first among you must be slave of all. For the Son of Man came not to be served but to serve" (Mark 10:43-45). A large dose of humility is a great antidote for the pride that sometimes afflicts us.

Let me tell you about fear

"I sought the Lord, and he answered me, /

and delivered me from all my fears."

Psalm 34:4

During my thirty-five years in ministry, I have been asked many times if I ever get anxious before I preach. My answer is always the same, "There has never been a time when I have spoken publicly that I haven't felt a little anxious." However, my anxiety reached an unfamiliar level when my nine-year-old niece asked me to speak to the International Club at her elementary school. My assignment was to give a forty-minute talk on Zimbabwe, Africa, at the end of the school day to seventy third, fourth, and fifth graders.

Over the weeks leading up to the presentation, my anxiety turned into actual terror. My conversation with myself went something like this: "I have never stood before a room full of elementary-aged students to speak for more than fifteen minutes, much less forty minutes. How am I supposed to keep them interested for that length of time, especially after they have been sitting in the classroom all day? I am sure that not even teachers who have been trained to teach these students would volunteer for such an assignment. These kids will eat me alive. My niece will be so embarrassed by my failure that she will never speak to me again. After this disastrous presentation, my sister, who is an outstanding teacher, will deny that she is related to me. I have to find an excuse for why I can't speak at the International Club." Fear of failure is a powerful force. Irrational thoughts and emotional paralysis are fruits of such fear.

Scripture teaches that "perfect love casts out fear" (1 John 4:18). As soon as I got to my niece's classroom, she was there to help me set up for the presentation. Before she pitched in, however, she gave me a big hug and said, "Thanks." At that moment, it became crystal clear to me that my performance would have no impact whatsoever on our love for each other. It was as if she had hugged the anxiety right out of me. God does the same for us. The psalmist declares, "I sought the Lord, and he answered me, / and delivered me from all my fears" (Ps 34:4). God's love for us is unconditional. It is not tied to our performance. God's perfect love through Christ squeezes out all our fears no matter how big or small. We have to simply welcome the embrace.

To run away or to stay

"I have fought the good fight, I have finished the race, I have kept the faith."

2 Timothy 4:7

Upon reading reports some years ago about the cries for freedom from thousands of protesters in the streets of Egypt and Libya, I was reminded of an encounter I had with a businessman in Zimbabwe, Africa. He spoke with great concern about the enormous political, social, and economic crisis facing his country. The system of government was ineffective to say the least. Unemployment was over 80 percent. Inflation was out of control. The crime rate was growing rapidly. Schools and colleges were closing for lack of funding. Medical clinics were low on supplies in the midst of a cholera epidemic. There were no easy answers as to how to turn around the steep decline of the once powerful and productive nation he called home. Many of his friends and neighbors had lost all hope for recovery and had fled the country. He and his wife, both having a deep faith, prayed about what they should do. His words, spoken with great passion and conviction, continue to echo in my head and touch my heart. He said, "My wife and I decided that we had two choices for responding to what was taking place in our nation. We could run away from all the problems by moving to another country, or we could stay and be a part of the solution. We have chosen to stay."

Jesus chose to go to the Garden of Gethsemane to talk with God about the most important decision he would ever make. He was about to decide whether he would run away from the heavy burden that had been placed upon him to address the sins of the world. Or he would decide to stay the course and be a part of the divine solution to the human condition of isolation and alienation. We read in Matthew that he threw himself down with his face to the ground and prayed, "My Father, if it is possible, let this cup pass from me; yet not what I want, but what you want" (Matt 26:39). Jesus chose to stay the course.

As followers of Jesus, we have a responsibility to reach out to the least, the last, and the lost to bring them into the divine community. Often, we are tempted to run from our obligation, especially when the price of fulfilling God's purpose is high. There is a cost to following Jesus. There is a price to be paid for standing up for what is right, just, and loving in the eyes of God. We can run away from the call to discipleship, or we can stay the course laid out by God and fight the good fight, run the race, and keep the faith (see 2 Tim 4:7). We have been given the freedom to choose. But we experience true personal freedom only when we choose the divine path, chosen by Jesus and the Zimbabwean businessman and his wife. We must make the choice each day to either run from the problems of the world or face them, seeking to be part of a divine solution. What choices are you making?

Mothers seem to know things

"Mary treasured all these words and pondered them in her heart."

Luke 2:19

I always thought my mom was wise beyond her years. She just seemed to know when I had not brushed my teeth, not completed my homework, or not finished my chores. She had a way of figuring out when I was going through a rough time with friends or when something significant was troubling me. Over time, I have come to believe that most mothers have this capacity to peer into our hearts in a way no one else has.

Maybe this is because moms have the God-given gift of pondering. The shepherds who had been tending their flocks by night told Mary and Joseph all that they had heard about Jesus from the heavenly host of angels. Then the Gospel of Luke records, "Mary treasured all these words and pondered them in her heart" (Luke 2:19).

The word ponder means to reflect, meditate, thoroughly consider, weigh carefully, or study. My mom had a unique ability to ponder confusing, challenging, or tragic situations, and then put them into perspective. Her perspective was always shaped by her faith in the steadfast love of God through Christ.

Back in the 1930s, a tornado touched down in Gurdon, Arkansas, during the night. My mom's house, where she, her sister, her two brothers, and parents were sleeping, was completely destroyed. After much reflection, she wrote this poem about that life-shaping event. In light of the storm damage that has ravaged the South in recent years, I believe that this is an appropriate time to share my mom's perspective on the Gurdon tornado.

He carried me out of
a storm that night
After waking with the
rain in my face.
Mother was crying—
the house is gone
And the night was
black as ink.
He picked me up—
I was heavy
And began a walk
without eyes.
Someone stepped thru
a glass window
That fell as the walls
came down—
Watch out for the wires
that snapped
As the dreadful thing
passed by.

He was strong and
calm and steady.
And I felt at peace
in his arms.
As he carried me out
of the storm that night
With the help and the
strength of God.
JH

That tornado was not the last time that my mom was carried out of a storm by arms that were strong and steady. The arms of God carried Mom from the storm of colon cancer years ago into God's heavenly kingdom where peace and steadfast love reign supreme. She knew the Lord was there to help in times of need.

I thank my mom for the strength of her arms and voice of faith that brought great calm and peace to my life. Above all, I thank the Lord for the gift of my mom, a "ponderer," who brought the perspective of the steadfast love of God to all the challenges that life has to offer.

Running, but going **nowhere**

"Who will rescue me...? Thanks be to God through Jesus Christ our Lord!"

Romans 7:24-25

Caleb, our hundred-pound, black Labrador Retriever, likes to plant himself on the ottoman in our family room. The problem is that he is so big he doesn't fit; parts of him hang over on all sides.

After work, I plopped down in my easy chair, and Caleb balanced himself on the ottoman. Suddenly, Caleb's nemesis—"the squirrel"—appeared in the backyard. Caleb immediately dropped his front legs over the edge of the ottoman, and his back legs came down over the opposite end. He proceeded to run at full speed toward the back door; however, his stomach was stuck on high center and his paws weren't touching the ground. He was running, but he was going nowhere. He was stuck, perplexed, and looked up at me for help.

In his letter to the Romans, the apostle Paul writes about getting stuck on his spiritual journey. He finds himself unable to get off high center when it comes to sin, aptly describing sin as "being full of himself" (see Rom 7:14 THE MESSAGE). Paul wants to move forward in his relationship with Christ but instead is simply running in place. He describes his predicament in verses 18-24: "I realize that I don't have what it takes. I can will it, but I can't do it.... My decisions, such as they are, don't result in actions.... I've tried everything and nothing helps. I'm at the end of my rope. Is there no one who can do anything for me?"

Paul then answers his own question about how to get unstuck: "The answer, thank God, is that Jesus Christ can and does" (Rom 7:25a THE MESSAGE). For Paul, Jesus had reached into his life through death on the cross and the resurrection to free Paul from being stuck on the high center of sin. Through the actions of Christ, Paul experienced freedom "to serve God with all my heart and mind" (v. 25b). The same is true for those of us who are stuck on the high center of self-centeredness, or in Paul's terms, "being full of ourselves."

Caleb, who was languishing on the ottoman, looked over at me pleading for help. I reached down, picked him up, and set him on solid ground; he was free to run again. In much the same way, when we cry for help, Jesus reaches down, picks us up, and frees us from being full of ourselves in order that we might become full of the love of God. Then, we can spend our days running to help others become unstuck in the name of Christ.

The day Henrietta got lost

"Which one of you, having a hundred sheep and losing one of them, does not leave the ninety-nine… and go after the one that is lost until he finds it?"

Luke 15:4

We had told our eleven-year-old daughter many times before that she could not take her pet hamster, Henrietta, to church with her. However, Erin was not the kind of child who asked permission. She was perfectly content, instead, to beg for forgiveness after the deed. Without our noticing, Erin had managed to slip Henrietta into her purse just as she and her mother walked out the front door one Sunday morning to drive to church.

After preaching, I was standing in my office changing out of my pastor's robe into my coat when a good friend and Sunday School teacher stuck her head through the door to inform me that she needed my help. Following her down the hallway to the education wing of our church, I was told that Erin's hamster, Henrietta, was lost. Further conversation revealed that in a bold attempt to escape bondage, Henrietta had managed to chew her way out of Erin's purse and was now lost in the church building. In an all-out effort by members and staff of our church, we frantically looked everywhere for one scared, lost pet hamster.

Jesus taught that just as we put all our effort into finding Henrietta, it is even more urgent and vital that we who are followers of Jesus search diligently for anyone who has lost faith and hope. Upon finding that one lost soul no apologies will be required, only celebration.

Lost now found.

The grand slam that wasn't

"[T]hose who sow righteousness get a true reward."

Proverbs 11:18

In May 2012, Mitch Moreland, a Texas Ranger first baseman and sometimes outfielder, hit his first major league grand slam home run against the Oakland A's. Yet, according to the rules of major league baseball, it never happened. Since the game was rained out before the end of four-and-a-half innings, Mitch's third inning heroics never officially took place. (By major league rules, four-and-a-half innings is the minimum number of innings for an official game. If the home team is not ahead at the end of that time, the minimum number of innings is five.) The game was canceled. All statistics were erased, and the game would be played over, from the start, at a later date. I wonder how Mitch Moreland must have felt about this turn of events. If only the rain had held off for a few more batters, his feat would have gone down in the official record books as a highlight of his major league career. Isn't it time for a change in the rules of major league baseball that would allow the statistics of any rain-shortened game, no matter the number of innings played, to be entered into the record books?

This injustice prompted me to think of all the heroic acts of faith that have gone unrecorded and, therefore, unnoticed throughout the years. How often did a courageous word spoken by Jesus transform a life, yet the event was never officially recorded in any of the four Gospels? Throughout the history of the church, how many times has an individual or a community of faith taken a bold stand for Christ that significantly shaped the future of Christendom, but due to circumstances that historic moment was never recorded for posterity?

Does it matter that, over the years, countless grand slams have been hit on behalf of a baseball team or on behalf of the love of Christ, but never made the record books? Of course not! Just ask Mitch Moreland. Yes, it would have been nice if the grand slam had been official. It could have helped his team to an official win. Whether recorded or not, however, what Mitch Moreland did that day mattered. It mattered that Mitch realized that, without a doubt, he had the God-given ability to make a significant contribution to helping his team reach its goals. For Mitch's teammates, as well as for those of us sitting in the stands, his unofficial grand slam gave us insight into what this team was capable of accomplishing together (a grand slam can occur only if three players manage to reach and stay on base before a batter hits a home run).This special moment gave the team and fans tremendous hope and confidence that more heroic moments were in store for the Rangers.

Join me, today, in celebrating all the people who have hit a grand slam for Christ yet never made it into the record books. We know that what they have done matters to Christ and to the building of God's kingdom. We also know that their heroics were possible only by the grace of God through the gift of faith. We benefit each day from the strong foundation of faith that they have anonymously built. Because of their unrecorded heroics, we are capable, by the grace of God, of new record-setting feats. Yet what these nameless heroes have taught us is what really matters is that God's name, not ours, be written down in the only record book that really counts—the heart (see Jer 31:33).

Instability in the air

"The Lord is my light and my salvation; /
whom shall I fear?"

Psalm 27:1

The wind was blowing so hard that the American flag was hanging on by only one eyelet. The dark clouds above us were moving in a circular motion with intermittent flashes of lightning illuminating the sky. John and I were at the Chicago White Sox vs. Texas Rangers baseball game at the ballpark in Arlington during the last week of May. More fans were watching the foreboding weather than the plays on the field. Suddenly, the person seated next to John and me announced that a tornado was sighted close to his house just four miles from the stadium.

The ballpark announcer told everyone to move from the top deck to one of the lower deck fan areas because of strong winds. Then the rain came. The wind blew even harder. Sirens could be heard in the distance announcing severe weather. Fans started emptying their seats and moving to the lowest level breezeways. My wife called my cell and said that there was a possible tornado headed from Fort Worth and that it should arrive at our location in about five minutes. I believe that my ten-year-old niece Callie, talking to her mom, accurately summarized what my son John and I were thinking at the moment: "Mom," she said, "I don't mean to hurt anyone's feelings or to say anything bad. But that's a stupid place to be tonight."

We spent the next few minutes attempting to find the safest place in the stadium to take cover. At first, we were simply under an overhang to protect us from the rain. Then, as the wind picked up, we went out to the walkway. The tornado warning prompted us to move into a very narrow covered walkway area. When my wife called about the potential tornado heading our way from Fort Worth, we moved to the other side of the stadium. Finally, thousands of us were led out onto the field and into a tunnel that took us under the stadium. Just as the last person entered the tunnel, the wind picked up and hail began pelting the field. No matter where John and I found shelter, the question in my mind was whether we were totally safe from the direct hit of a tornado. I concluded that there was no completely safe place from physical harm in that geographical location.

There is a spiritual location to which our hearts and minds can go to find refuge and strength regardless of the ferocity of the storms we are facing. One of the psalmists found that place in a time of need:

> The Lord is my light and my salvation;
> whom shall I fear?
> The Lord is the stronghold of my life;
> of whom shall I be afraid?

For he will hide me in his shelter
in the day of trouble;
he will set me high on a rock.
Be strong, and let your heart take courage;
wait for the Lord.

Ps 27:1,5,14

Our one true refuge and strength when instability is in the air is the Lord our God. So the best place to be in the midst of a storm is not a geographical location but a spiritual location, the place called faith. I believe the writer of Psalm 27 is suggesting that prayer is the best place to start when looking for shelter in time of need. Reflecting on our experience at the ballpark, I believe the psalmist is right!

2020 - The year we all helped each other

"[O]ne will lift up the other."

Ecclesiastes 4:10

Our group of St. Andrew Helping Hands volunteers noticed the words above on a poster on a telephone pole outside Lockhart Smokehouse in the Bishop Arts District of Dallas as we purchased barbecue meals to serve the emergency room personnel at Methodist Dallas Medical Center.

The hospital staff gathered in front of the emergency room entrance to receive the meals provided in gratitude for their selfless work to protect and save lives from COVID-19. As we delivered these meals on behalf of the St. Andrew family and Lockhart, random drivers passed by the hospital honking their horns and rolling down their car windows to shout words of heartfelt thanks for the sacrificial efforts of the emergency room staff.

While hospital beds continued to fill with COVID-19 patients, I prayed that we would be aware of the fact that it would take all of us working to help each other in 2020 to stop the spread of the debilitating and sometimes deadly virus. Wearing masks, social distancing, and washing our hands were our weapons to contain and defeat this pandemic. My prayer was that we would fervently use this weaponry to protect the potential victims of COVID-19, to honor the sacrifices of our courageous health workers, and to affirm the good news of the gospel that "God did not send his Son into the world to condemn the world, but in order that the world might be saved through him" (John 3:17). As disciples who are called to serve as the hands and feet of Christ, God was now counting upon us to love, serve, and save one another (John 3:16). As members of the St. Andrew family, we joined together to do our part.

In every time of trial, help us, Lord, to help each other.

Somebody doesn't love a wall

"For [Jesus] is our peace; in his flesh he has made both groups into one and has broken down the dividing wall, that is, the hostility between us."

Ephesians 2:14

When the Lord Almighty looks down from heaven at the earth, God must think that we humans have a love affair with walls. Walls are erected everywhere you look. You see walls separating buildings, backyards, cities, and nations. They are made of wood, brick, concrete, metal, and barbed wire. Some walls are built to keep others outside while others are designed to keep people inside.

Upon closer inspection, we find invisible walls that have stood for centuries, with new ones being built every day. These walls are often constructed from the materials of fear, prejudice, and animosity. Walls like this originate from disagreements and misunderstandings. Sometimes, they rise up out of a desire for power or control.

The first line of Robert Frost's poem, "Mending Wall," reads, "[Somebody] there is that doesn't love a wall." For those in the family of faith, that "somebody" is Jesus himself. Jesus made it his mission in life to tear down walls separating us from God and from one another. Sometimes he simply chipped away at these barriers a little at a time by dining with the "despised" like the tax collector Zacchaeus, or offering words of hope to an "outcast" like the Samaritan woman who had come to draw water from a well.

Other times, Jesus' actions had the effect of a wrecking ball. When Jesus dramatically turned over the tables of the money-changers in the temple courtyard, he was dismantling the wall that made it difficult for the "have-nots" to join the "haves" for worship there. Jesus' ultimate act of redemption was removing the dividing wall of sin and death through his death on the cross and resurrection.

As the apostle Paul, who himself was reconciled to God and the family of faith by Jesus' crucifixion and resurrection, writes to the church in Rome, "we, who are many, are one body in Christ" (Rom 12:5). This is Paul's way of saying that, despite differences and disagreements, in Christ the walls of fear, animosity, and prejudice are toppled. "(Somebody) there is that doesn't love a wall," and that "somebody" is Jesus. As followers of Jesus Christ, that "somebody" now includes you and me.

Putting on the life jacket called grace

"For by grace you have been saved through faith, and this is not your own doing; it is the gift of God."

Ephesians 2:8

I look back now and ask, "Whatever possessed me?"

Two of my sons and I had booked a three-hour whale-watching expedition on a small boat. We were just underway on our Indian Ocean adventure when a crew member mentioned that I might be more comfortable taking off my life jacket. "The waves should be subsiding the farther out into the ocean we go," he said. My first response was, "I'm all right. I'll just leave it on." A few minutes later he mentioned again that I would be much more comfortable without the life jacket. I said, "Okay," and proceeded to take it off.

Maybe twenty minutes passed before the wind began to pick up. The swells grew to at least four feet high. The boat was being batted about by the waves, much like a child might splash large quantities of water on a toy plastic boat in the bathtub in an effort to sink it. Now, I was attempting to hold onto the railing of the boat with one hand while I was holding my camera in the other in anticipation that a humpback whale would breach at any moment. At this point, my sons, Stephen and John, began to sound like parents. They were saying things like, "Dad, where is your life jacket? You need to put it on! Put down the camera and hold on with both hands!"

Then, without warning, not one but two adult humpback whales breached the water, side by side. It was an amazing sight to behold. I had never seen anything like it and probably will never witness anything to compare to it again. I attempted to take a picture, but another wave rocked the boat and I lost my balance. Not only did I not get a picture, I lost my grip, and my sons caught me as I was thrown halfway across the boat's observation deck. Later, my boys told my sister and my ten-year-old niece about the harrowing experience. My niece asked my adult sons, "Where was the adult supervision?" Their response was, "Nonexistent!"

Looking back now, I still can't believe I took the life jacket off. I know better, and I never would have given consent to my sons removing theirs. It is well known that a life jacket is a proven commodity when it comes to keeping people safe and saving lives. But it won't protect you unless you are wearing it.

Ephesians 2:8 reads, "For by grace you have been saved through faith, and this is not your own doing; it is the gift of God." The writer is saying to the church in Ephesus that God's grace is a life jacket that God hands to us through the work of Jesus Christ. Don't reject this proven commodity! The Lord's amazing grace protects and saves us from drowning in a sea of loneliness and meaningless existence. So, by faith, take and wear this jacket of grace daily. It's when we waiver in our faith that we are tempted to succumb to outside pressures to remove this life jacket and face life's rough seas alone.

Through participation in Christian service, we are called to hand others the life jacket called grace and to help them keep it cinched tight so we can weather the storms of life. We will find ourselves in tremendous peril without it.

A new source of fuel

"Bear one another's burdens, and in this way you will fulfill the law of Christ."

Galatians 6:2

Sharon and I traveled to Magnolia, Arkansas, for a Hasley family reunion. We spent the night, then packed up the car the next day to come back to Plano. I was waving goodbye to the Hasley clan as I turned the key to start the car. The car did not start. Continuing to wave goodbye, I turned the key again. The engine sounded as if it wanted to start, but ultimately it did not. Several more times I turned the key, thinking that the engine was going to turn over. There was no reason it shouldn't start, I thought. The car was relatively new. The day before, it had made the four-and-a-half-hour trip to Magnolia with no trouble. I had recently taken the car in for an oil change and a general checkup. I had been told that all was in good working order.

Unnoticed by me, my brother-in-law, Jeff, disappeared during my futile efforts to get the car started. When he reappeared, he was carrying a five-gallon container. He walked up to the back left side of the car, unscrewed the gas cap, put a funnel in place and began pouring gasoline. He emptied the container. He removed the funnel and screwed on the cap. He looked at me and said, “Now, try starting the car.” I turned the key and immediately heard the purr of the engine. Sporting a bright red complexion, I continued waving goodbye as Sharon and I pulled out of the driveway and headed home.

There are times along our faith journey when we wake up to discover that, despite our best efforts, we don’t seem to be able to move forward. We keep trying things to get our spiritual engine running, things that have helped in the past, only to find that we are not budging. In those moments, it is a phenomenal blessing to have a member of the family of faith standing nearby who cares about us, who encourages growth in our relationship with the Lord, who is willing to help us assess our spiritual condition, and who extends a helping hand when we are stuck. They can pour fuel into our souls by providing words of guidance and encouragement, by prayer, or simply by listening to us with a compassionate spirit.

To have so **much**, yet only wanting **more**

"But strive first for the kingdom of God, and his righteousness, and all these things will be given to you as well."

Matthew 6:33

Upon his return from a St. Andrew mission trip to build a house for a homeless family, Eric shared the following thought with his mom. He reflected, "They [the homeless family] have so little and yet are so happy. We have so much, and we only want more." This fourteen-year-old boy had gained a profound insight into one of the greatest spiritual challenges that our society faces today.

We spend much of our lives focusing our time, energy, and resources on acquiring more, bigger, better, and newer things. There is no sin in having money and wealth. Possessions and money are morally neutral. They can be used for evil or good. What is evil is the belief that the acquisition of more belongings is our primary purpose in life. Sin is convincing ourselves that having more possessions will increase our joy and happiness in this life. Therefore, we are shocked and surprised when our constant need for more and better results in a decrease of joy, while increasing stress. Jesus taught, "One's life does not consist in the abundance of possessions" (Luke 12:15).

As Jesus said, "But strive first for the kingdom of God and his righteousness, and all these things will be given to you as well" (Matt 6:33). If we put God first in our lives, the "things [that] will be given" to us will not be material in nature, but spiritual. We will be blessed with a purpose for living: to serve God by serving others. Furthermore, dedication to serving God and others will lead us to a life of simplicity and generosity. Along this spiritual pathway, we will receive God-given joy and contentment that lasts, no matter the state of our worldly possessions.

Can-do confidence and a wave of the towel

"I can do all things through him who strengthens me."

Philippians 4:13

As my son, John, and I entered the ballpark in Arlington, each fan was handed a towel adorned with the team logo. The Texas Rangers baseball team was counting on fan support, shown by cheering and waving the towels, to help lift them to victory in Game 5 of the 2011 World Series. The game was a nail-biter. We were tied 2–2 going into the bottom of the eighth inning. Since the sixth inning, the fan on our left had used the towel to cover her eyes. She was so anxious about the outcome she could not bring herself to watch. I fully understood her high stress level. She wanted those who were watching to tell her what was happening. The fans on our right had been standing, cheering, and waving their towels since the sixth inning. We were all shouting "Na-po-li!" as Mike Napoli stepped up to the plate for the Rangers in the bottom of the eighth. He proceeded to hit a double that brought in two more runs. The hit proved to be the game winner. The crowd went wild. The person on my left finally removed her towel from her face revealing huge tears of relief and joy running down her cheeks.

What I experienced that night at the ballpark characterized what I believe are two quite different worldviews about life's outcomes. The first is based on the belief that we have no influence over what happens to us or others in this life; therefore, we are tempted to just cover our eyes and wish for the best. The second view says that we are able, through words and/or actions, to influence outcomes, regarding our own lives and the lives of others.

Scripture teaches us that there is a third worldview to consider. We hear this outlook expressed by Paul in his letter to the Philippians, "I can do all things through him who strengthens me" (4:13). In this faith-centered view, what we say and do when undergirded by the strength of God's peace has a tremendous influence over our ability to shape future outcomes. When it comes to fan support, maybe our best choice is to wave a towel in support of Christ who strengthens us all. To do so is guaranteed to be a game changer.

A multiplication of blessings

"God is love."

1 John 4:8

Over the years I have been blessed, along with my sons, Stephen, John, and Will, with a remarkable number of opportunities around sports to spend time together. A variety of sporting events have brought us together including baseball, basketball, football, golf, rugby, marathons, WWF wrestling, monster truck rallies, and hurling (a lacrosse-like Gaelic sport). Each time one of my three boys announced their wedding plans, I was immensely happy for them. However, I am embarrassed to admit that I was also a little concerned about how this change might impact our ability to gather around sports.

I quickly discovered my apprehension was unwarranted. Instead of diminishing our blessings, they were significantly increased with the additions of three fantastic daughters-in-law: Will's wife, Amanda, Stephen's wife, Amanda, and John's wife, Ananya. Our sporting interests were definitely not diminished. Rather they were enhanced by my daughters-in-law's interests in field hockey, whitewater rafting, hiking, cross-country skiing, cricket, and more.

One daughter-in-law, joined by my granddaughters, recently won the NCAA March Madness College Basketball Hasley Family Bracket Challenge. Another daughter-in-law, for the sake of my personal health, encouraged me to invite a friend (I interpreted "friend" to mean "competitor") to begin fast walking around the block at least once each day. Then, a third daughter-in-law actually agreed to set aside space on a living room bookshelf for a few Major League Baseball player bobble head dolls.

However, what has impressed me most about my daughters-in-law is how they model for Will, Stephen, John, and me what love is. Love is the act of expressing interest in the things that bring joy to another. Amanda, Amanda, and Ananya's modeling of selfless love for my sons is working. My youngest son is learning from his wife, Amanda, how to communicate to his three daughters his interest in what brings them joy. Stephen is learning how to expand his own interest in the wonder and beauty of the great outdoors which brings tremendous joy to his wife, Amanda. John is learning how to cook and to garden which are activities that bring joy to Ananya.

Love multiplied has blessed us all.

Redefining greatness

"This is my commandment: that you love one another as I have loved you. No one has greater love than this, to lay down one's life for one's friends."

John 15:12-13

A few years ago, I attended a memorial service for Don Hubbard, my high school football and track coach from 1967 through 1970. When the worship service began, First United Methodist Church of Magnolia, Arkansas, was packed with family, friends, administrators, teachers, and coaches from the Magnolia public schools and around the state, along with former athletes Don had coached.

As I listened to one of the high school principals list Coach Hubbard's many accomplishments, including three state championships in football (with undefeated seasons in 1968 and 1972), Arkansas High School Coach of the Year, and Arkansas Athletic Director of the Year, I realized to my surprise that I could not remember one score from the games I played under Coach Hubbard. I could not even remember the score of one game from our 1968 undefeated season when I played.

However, I could recall the multiple times Coach Hubbard called to check on me after I suffered a concussion in a game against the Hope Bobcats. I remembered how he was there for my mom, my sisters, and me when my father died suddenly of a massive heart attack at age fifty-three. I remember that Coach asked me to officiate his marriage to Jennifer in Cox Chapel in Dallas. When I was asked to come home to Magnolia to preach in my home church, Coach Hubbard and Jennifer were there despite Don's battle with an acute form of palsy that affected both his balance and speech. Afterward during our visit, he handed me a photograph from a game I had played back in 1969.

At the memorial service, it dawned on me that most of us who had gathered to remember Don Hubbard were not there because of his wins on a football field or at a track meet. We were there because we were all recipients of his leadership, love, and support over the years. At some point in his life he had clearly decided that a scoreboard would not be the defining factor when it came to determining his contribution toward making this world a better place. Instead, he chose to focus his life's work on investing in relationships. Those of us gathered that Saturday afternoon to honor Coach's memory were a living testimony to his success.

An every-Sunday worshiper, Coach Hubbard was very familiar with these words from Jesus: "love one another as I have loved you" (John 15:12).

All for an angel

"The angel said to them, 'Do not be afraid; for see—I am bringing you good news of great joy for all the people."

Luke 2:10

Will and Amanda, my youngest son and daughter-in-law, invited me to come to Crozet, Virginia, to attend my fifteen-year-old granddaughter Angel's school play. With a heavy work schedule in front of me, I thought there was no way I could attend. But at the same moment, I thought there was no way I was going to miss Angel's performance as Juliet in "Romeo and Juliet". I promptly bought a ticket for a flight to Charlotte, North Carolina, where I would catch another flight to the Charlottesville, Virginia airport, which is twenty minutes from Crozet.

What I did not anticipate on the day of my departure was a flight delay. I missed my connecting flight to Charlottesville. The only option was to fly to Richmond, rent a car, and drive 1 1/2 hours to Crozet. When I stepped up to the car rental counter in Richmond, I was informed that the highway had iced over due to the rain and cold. After almost three hours in stop-and-go traffic, I arrived in Crozet. I rented a room over a downtown bakery with the hope of getting a good night's sleep.

At approximately 2:00 a.m., I was awakened to the sound of two smoke alarms in my room activated by a power outage throughout Crozet. I pulled my pillow over my head to muffle the sound. It didn't work. I got up to check a few emails until the electricity returned. I checked emails until 5:30 a.m. at which time the lights came on and the alarms stopped buzzing. By then, it was time to get dressed and to spend the day playing with my granddaughters Emogene, age three, and Joy, who was eight months old and their mom, Amanda.

After my long, tense traveling day, followed by a sleepless night and a non-stop play day, it is an understatement to say that I was struggling to keep my eyes open from the moment the curtain came up for Angel's play until the final bow. In fact, Will had to give me an elbow in the side just in time for me to open my eyes to catch Angel's balcony scene as Juliet. Angel was such a blessing to watch as she put her heart into her amazing performance.

The best moment of all came when, with a huge smile on her face, Angel gave me a big hug and said, "Papaw, thanks so much for coming to my play." My Angel brought tremendous joy to my heart that night due to an extra helping of God's grace coupled with a little effort on my part. As the old saying goes, "Some things in life are well worth the effort; it's just a matter of learning what those things are." The shepherds on the hillside came to understand, as did I that night in Crozet, that being there for one another is always well worth our effort—just as our Lord is always there for us.

Blessed by unexpected outcomes

"I will put my trust in him (God)...
I and the children whom God has given me."

Hebrews 2:13

Several years ago, a few days after Christmas, Sharon, Erin, our sons, and I traveled to Magnolia, Arkansas, to spend some time with extended family. I remember walking into my sister and brother-in-law's living room to find next to the Christmas tree a child-sized basketball goal with jewelry hanging on the rim. This was a clear sign that Callie, their five-year-old daughter, would grow up to have a mind of her own regarding her future. That God-given mind of hers has recently led her to declare Bio-Medical Engineering as her major field of study at Texas A&M University and to choose playing the cello as her favorite extra-curricular activity.

Having raised children of my own I have come to realize, as have Barbara and Jeff, that there is one thing we can count on in this life: to expect the unexpected. The Lord God has not placed us on this earth to control outcomes, but instead to use our lives as instruments of divine grace and love, trusting the outcomes to God. I have personally found this to be easier said than done. However, when I am able to release control of outcomes, true joy abounds.

A little more "March Madness" please

"He had been instructed in the way of the Lord; and he spoke with burning enthusiasm and taught accurately the things concerning Jesus."

Acts 18:25

Madness, defined as wild excitement, grows rapidly each year in anticipation of the tipoff of the NCAA Men's and Women's Basketball Tournaments. Winners and losers are projected. Fans frantically complete their brackets. (I know this because my wife Sharon, my sons, their families, and I fill out our brackets to compete against one another for bragging rights, as do members of our St. Andrew staff.) Trash talk over winners and losers can be overheard in hallways, at the coffee bar, and during mealtime. Employers complain about the loss of productivity in the workplace because of wild and excessive preoccupation with this college basketball tournament, concluding with the crowning of a champion in early April.

Some might say enough is enough when it comes to such madness. But I say let's have more "madness" when it comes to our faith. Let's increase our intensity, excitement, and enthusiasm in the spring and throughout the year when we direct our hearts and minds toward remembering and celebrating the presence of the Risen Christ in our lives. I believe that:

—if we choose to direct as much energy toward studying and analyzing the last week of Jesus' life leading up to his death and resurrection, as we do in preparation for our March Madness brackets… and

—if we spend as much time in prayer and meditation considering what Holy Week says about who God is and who we are called to be as his children, as we do thinking about our Final Four predictions… and

—if we are accused of being fanatics when it comes to our Easter celebration of the victory of a crucified and risen Savior over sin and death, as much as sports fans are accused of being fanatical for their teams…

then our "madness" will be time, energy, and enthusiasm well spent. A difference between "Holy Week Madness" and NCAA March Madness is that the excitement does not end the first of April with the presentation of a trophy. Instead, "Holy Week Madness" transforms us in such a way that our wild excitement over what God through Christ has done to save us has a lasting effect on the way we view the world and the way we live our lives. And better yet, by God's grace, such "Holy Week Madness" will someday be pervasive enough to change an entire world. Now that kind of "madness" is truly divine!

Landing the big one

"Follow me, and I will make you fish for people."

Matthew 4:19

Over the years, my fishing trips have resulted in few fish but a lot of big talk about the ones that got away. However, on June 16, 2012, off the coast of Sanibel Island, Florida, my son John and I had an experience that was quite different.

Our good friend, John Hamilton, had arranged a two-day tarpon fishing trip for all of us. We had never fished for tarpon. As a matter of fact, the only tarpon we had ever seen was on a sport fishing channel.

On our first day, we saw a few splashes in the Gulf of Mexico that our fishing guide identified as tarpon. However, he noted that these tarpon were stragglers. According to our guide, who had been fishing these waters for thirty-three years, the schools of tarpon had left two weeks earlier. With this disappointing news I adjusted my expectations for the outcome of our fishing trip.

That first day we caught three, small, black-tipped sharks, and a lemon shark. However, we spent most of the day watching osprey dive into the gulf for mackerel. We also saw a few frigate birds and an enormous loggerhead turtle.

As we sped into the harbor at the end of the day, our

guide reported that the next day's forecast called for higher winds, which would make for choppy open water. He strongly suggested that we would have better luck fishing inland for trout. I had adjusted my expectations about this fishing experience, but my son clearly had not. John turned to me with another suggestion. He argued that, in addition to seeing our friends, the Hamiltons, we had come to Florida to fish for tarpon. He wanted to spend our final day of deep-sea fishing attempting to catch one. So we did.

The waves were a little higher the next day as we fished for live bait in the channel. However, we were successful catching a good number of bait fish with pieces of shrimp. John Hamilton named one of those bait fish Jack and commented that Jack was our secret weapon.

We went back to the area off the coast of Sanibel Island where he had spotted signs of tarpon the day before. After more than an hour with no bites, he moved us closer to the shore. As our guide rebated the hooks, John Hamilton suggested that he use the bait named Jack to lure the tarpon. A short time later, a sixty-five-plus pound tarpon hit Jack. Our guide yelled, "Tarpon!" He grabbed the rod and reel mounted at the stern and handed it to John. The tarpon, while jumping and diving frantically away from our boat, threw the hook out of its mouth and was lost.

Then our guide reviewed for all of us the procedure for landing a tarpon: bow (lower the rod) when the fish jumps out of the water and lift the rod while reeling when the fish re-enters the water. He told us that he had seen few tarpon as active as this young one that got away and that there was no guarantee that we could have landed him even with the best technique. My son John had fallen silent. This had been our only tarpon action in one-and-a-half days. John clearly felt like the rest of us that this may have been our one opportunity to land one.

Then, John Hamilton spoke up: "Let's put 'Jack II' on the hook." Within thirty minutes, the rod at the bow of the boat bent in half. The guide again yelled, "Tarpon!" My son jumped up and grabbed the rod and reel. At that moment the tarpon, which weighed no less than one-hundred-fifty pounds, jumped straight up out of the water. He was not more than thirty yards from the boat. Our jaws dropped. This was not a youngster. This was papa! I grabbed the fishing belt, and John Hamilton put it around my son's waist. John placed the handle of the fishing pole into the belt socket so that he could have ample leverage for the battle that would ensue. John Hamilton and I reeled in the other lines so that John could circle the boat as he fought the tarpon. I turned to John Hamilton and gave him a high five, thanking him for arranging this trip. "This is the best," I said, "to see the look of joy on my son's face when he hooks the big one!"

As John began his struggle to conquer this goliath, the boat captain noticed that the boat was listing. The small fishing boat had taken on a great deal of water on this windy day in the Gulf. As John Hamilton and I scooped ankle high water into buckets and threw it overboard, John battled the tarpon. The captain finally indicated that we had bailed enough water, and I stepped over to see how John was doing. He voiced concern that he was running out of line. At that moment, the tarpon jumped out of the water some one-hundred-fifty yards from the boat. The captain started the engine and headed the boat toward the fish.

John continued to bow, lift up on the reel, and crank while the rest of us continued to work to keep the boat afloat. I tried to speak to John, but he wouldn't respond. He was totally focused on bringing in the tarpon. I did take him water to keep him from becoming dehydrated. I held the bottle up to his mouth while he simultaneously drank and fought the fish. He eventually thanked me for serving as his cornerman (a reference to the man providing water and a towel for a boxer between rounds).

After approximately one hour and ten minutes, John brought the tarpon to the side of the boat. He was spent, both physically and emotionally. Yet I have never seen a bigger smile on his face. Our guide held the fish by the side of the boat so that we could take pictures. Then, after our guide removed a scale to serve as proof that John had landed the behemoth, we released the tarpon back into the water so that the mighty fish could fight another day.

Several of Jesus' first disciples were fishermen. They would have known the joy of a great catch! Jesus took that joy even deeper when he said to them, "Follow me, and I will make you fish for people" (Matt 4:19). I wonder if Jesus might have added (though unrecorded), "… while I serve as your guide and cornerman."

Left behind

"For the Son of Man came to seek out and to save the lost."

Luke 19:10

After attending Will and Amanda's joyous wedding in Charlottesville, Virginia, Sharon, Erin, and I were on the final leg of our drive home. We pulled over for a quick stop in Hazen, Arkansas. After filling up the gas tank, we jumped back into the car to continue our trip to Plano, Texas. As we pulled onto the highway, we realized that we were missing something (or, to be more specific, someone). We had left our college-aged daughter, Erin, at the service station. I tried calling her cell phone to tell her we would be right back. However, her ringtone could be heard coming from the back seat. Erin called us from the service station phone. Needless to say, our explanation for how we could have left her behind was not satisfactory, at least as far as she was concerned. Our singular focus on getting home resulted in a lack of focus on making sure that all of us were making the trip.

The Lord calls upon us to join God on a spiritual journey to become passionate servants. The destination is all-important, but just as vital to the Lord is making sure everyone is on the trip. This truth about the nature of Christ is highlighted in Matthew 18:12-14. We are told that the shepherd is willing to leave the ninety-nine sheep in order to find the one lost sheep. As Luke declares, "the Son of Man came to seek out and to save the lost" (Luke 19:10).

A core value for Jesus is to leave no one behind. Most of us who are a part of the community of faith would say that is our focus as well. However, other agendas sometimes result in diverting our attention away from this core value. We can find ourselves leaving others behind, even members of our own family, when traveling the pathway of faith. Jesus challenges us to see our personal spiritual journey as tied to the spiritual needs of those around us. We are called as a community to come home to a relationship with the Lord who is our Creator, Redeemer, and Shepherd. If we do not get in the car to take the journey of faith with Christ, the Lord will come to find us. The Lord chooses to leave no one behind.

Do you want to be right, or do you want to be happy?

He said, "Abba, Father, for you all things are possible; remove this cup from me; yet, not what I want, but what you want."

Mark 14:36

The title of this devotion is one of my wife's favorite quotations. It is especially relevant during March Madness. We both fill out our brackets for the Men's NCAA Basketball Tournament. Then, we follow the results.

From this friendly spousal competition I have gained some surprising yet invaluable knowledge. First of all, it is possible for your competition to select their teams based on the "cute factor" as pertaining to the team mascot (and players), school colors, or region of the country from which they come. Even if you have done extensive research yourself or used the knowledge of the most notable sports experts, these other methods have resulted in victory for my wife.

I have also noticed that the few times I have won, the victory celebration fell far short of what I expected. Have you ever heard the phrase "When Mama isn't happy, nobody is happy"? There is great truth to be found in this saying.

So my greatest lesson learned from our annual March Madness competition is that being bested by your wife is not the worst thing that can happen to you. On the several occasions when she has won, she wears a contagious smile that spreads from ear to ear. She often dances, harkening back to her drill team days. Furthermore, she can high five with the best of them. The good feeling engendered by her "astute" selection of winning college basketball teams lasts for quite some time.

So now I come back to one of Sharon's favorite quotations: "Do you want to be right, or do you want to be happy?" Right might feed our pride in the moment, but there is a much brighter future in happy.

There is a biblical parallel to my story. The religious leaders of Jesus' day insisted they had all the right answers when it came to the knowledge, interpretation, and observance of God's laws. Jesus came along and issued a direct challenge to their need to be right and in control when it came to spiritual matters. Basically, Jesus asked, "Which is your greater desire? Is it the desire to be right or is it the desire to experience the joy of surrendering your life and your will to God?"

Jesus answered his own question in a prayer he offered up to God in the Garden of Gethsemane: "… not what I want, but what you want" (Mark 14:36). Jesus found great joy in his choice to serve rather than to be served. Then, from a cross on hill, he challenged us to do the same.

He stood up for me

"We were reconciled to God through the death of his Son."

Romans 5:10

As a parent, you spend a great deal of time and effort providing for your children. When you do not believe they are being treated fairly, you are the first to stand up for them. What I did not anticipate as a parent was the day my children would stand up for me.

I was playing golf with my sons in Colorado. Evidently, there were signs posted to keep carts on the sidewalk or fairway to protect the native flora located in the rough. I did not notice the signs. In addition, I am a "social" golfer who has a great deal of difficulty keeping my golf ball in the fairway.

The course marshal spotted me driving the golf cart into the rough (protected area). The words he shouted cannot be repeated in devotional material. What I can report is what my sons shouted back to him: "That's our dad!" I was too far away to hear the rest of the conversation. However, the next thing I saw was the marshal driving away toward the next fairway. Now this may not seem like a big thing to some, but I was touched that, without hesitation, my sons stood up for me.

The only times I am more deeply touched by someone standing up on my behalf is during the Good Friday service held at our church. Through the power of scripture, music, and a message, we relive the death of Jesus on the cross delivering us from sin and death. I, along with hundreds of other worshipers, leave the Sanctuary, overwhelmed by the knowledge that Jesus was standing up for us when he died on the cross that day. Out of love for us, he gave his life that we might have life in him, free from the power of fear.

The question Jesus leaves for us to answer is, "Are we willing, without hesitation, to do the same for him by taking a stand for his children who are lost and without hope?"

The first pitch, part 1

"Jesus immediately reached out his hand and caught him, saying to him, 'You of little faith, why did you doubt?'"

Matthew 14:31

One Sunday afternoon, I delivered the ceremonial first pitch at the Frisco RoughRiders baseball game. The director of our St. Andrew Children's Ministry asked if I would like to have the honor. Throwing a ceremonial first pitch at a professional baseball game is on my bucket list of things to do before I leave this earth, so I jumped at the opportunity.

A few days later, however, when I began thinking about throwing a baseball sixty feet from the pitcher's mound over home plate into the glove of a professional catcher, doubt began to creep into my mind. Had my decision to do this been made too hastily? For instance, the thought that I had not thrown a baseball since I was in college (almost forty years ago!) started to gnaw away at me. Knowing there would be family and friends watching intently also began to work on my psyche. Finally, I realized that I have only one opportunity to get the ball over the plate. There is no "do-over" for ceremonial first pitches. So, that well-known expression began to occupy my thoughts: "I may have bitten off more than I can chew!"

Doubt about his ability to step up to his role as Jesus' disciple and loyal friend filled Peter's mind while he stood in a courtyard just outside the place where Jesus was on trial for his life. When asked if he was one of Jesus' followers, three times Peter denied that he even knew Jesus. Doubt and fear hijacked his voice.

Then there was Thomas, who doubted the resurrection of Jesus. When he finally saw the Risen Christ with the nail prints in his hands and the wound in his side, did it cross Thomas' mind that he may have "bitten off more than he could chew" when he chose to be a disciple of Jesus? However, when he gazed into the eyes of the Risen Lord while surrounded and supported by a community of fellow followers of Christ, faith overcame his fear and confidence replaced his doubt.

When was the last time doubt and fear overwhelmed your thoughts and took control of your actions and speech? Try allowing the amazing power of God's grace into your heart. Focus your thoughts on the Risen Christ while standing in the midst of a supportive community of faith called the church. If you do, I believe—with all of my heart, mind, soul, and strength—that the dark clouds of fear and doubt will be replaced by the light of Christ that brings faith, hope, and love into our lives.

I must say that my apprehension about the outcome of my ceremonial first pitch still lingered. I realized it was highly unlikely that I would be offered a minor league baseball contract after my pitching performance. However, I have no doubt that God will continue to extend an everlasting contract to play on God's team. The signature required on God's contract is belief in his only begotten Son, Jesus Christ. In Christ, we discover that we are freed from our greatest doubts and fears so that we might live faithfully and confidently in him. Now that is something worth celebrating with family and friends at a baseball park on Sunday afternoon, and particularly in worship on Saturday night or Sunday morning.

Breakfast with my **dad**

"Jesus said to them, 'Come and have breakfast.'"

John 21:12

The District Championship basketball game was in the final period with two minutes remaining. Two of our players had already fouled out. I was the last player left on the bench when the third player was called for a foul. He, too, had fouled out. My contribution over the next four minutes was two fouls and a missed shot. We had been up by five points when I entered the big game against our archrivals. We lost by one point. I felt I had let down my team.

My dad was at that Friday night game, not only because I was playing, but because he was superintendent of the Magnolia public schools. Little was said on the ride home. The next morning, he awakened me with, "Let's go downtown and have breakfast!"

This offer was unusual for at least two reasons. First, my dad rarely ate breakfast on Saturdays, and I usually slept in that one day of the week. Second, the only time we ever went out to eat was Sunday lunch or on very special occasions like birthdays or graduations. So our Saturday trip to the Chatterbox Restaurant, located just off the town square, was a big deal. I ordered my favorite: a huge stack of buttermilk pancakes. I do not remember now what was said over our breakfast. I do not believe that we even mentioned the game the night before. However, for more than forty years, I have cherished that breakfast with my dad, just the two of us eating out at a restaurant. It was a special treat. Somehow, my performance at a basketball game no longer seemed especially significant in the grand scheme of things. There would be many more special moments like this with my father, just waiting to be enjoyed.

After the disciples failed to stand by Jesus during his trial, flogging, and crucifixion, they must have felt that they had let down their Lord, teacher, and friend. In the midst of their pain, Jesus came to them by the Sea of Galilee and said, "Come and have breakfast." We are not told what was said during the breakfast. All we know is that Jesus and his disciples ate bread and fish together on the shore by the Sea of Galilee. The disciples must have realized at that moment that the world had not come to an end with the death of Jesus. Instead, Jesus' invitation to breakfast gave the disciples hope that there would be many special times ahead to be enjoyed in communion with the Risen Christ (see John 21:1-14).

Never underestimate the power of a good breakfast with someone you love. Afterward, the world looks a little brighter, and the future is more hopeful. By the way, you do not have to wait to be invited to breakfast. You can be the one who extends the invitation.

The first pitch, part 2

"The greatest of these is love."

1 Corinthians 13:13

Just a few days before the ceremonial first pitch at the Frisco RoughRiders baseball game, my eleven-year-old niece informed me that she had made three cards for me. Callie's plan was to give me two of the three at the ballpark.

Just before my pitch, she was going to give me the first card, which read, "Good Luck!" Then, based on the outcome of my throw, she would give me one of the two remaining cards. One card read, "Congratulations!" accompanied by the word "Hurrah!" repeated on the front of the card twenty times, and ending with the phrase, "Just couldn't stop at three cheers." Then, just in case the performance was short of stellar, the third card read, "Good Try!" On the front of this card were words from Winston Churchill: "Never, never, never, never give up," followed by words from Callie: "I'll never, never, never, never stop cheering for you."

I was reminded by Callie's cards that, no matter the result of my first-ever ceremonial first pitch (high on my bucket list), I already had the best life has to offer: the unconditional love of family and friends. The apostle Paul wrote, "And I will show you a more excellent way. If I speak in the tongues of mortals and angels, but do not have love, I am a noisy gong or a clanging cymbal.... Pursue love" (1 Cor 12:31b; 13:1; 14:1a). Translated, a perfect first pitch with all the accompanying accolades pales in comparison to Christlike love given and received.

My goal on Sunday afternoon was to throw a strike. After several prior practice sessions, I had faith and hope that I could accomplish my goal. However, the result was a rainbow sinker that was very low (as in short) and outside. Yet when I returned to the stands, I discovered that the best part was waiting for me there: a card created by Callie just for her Uncle Papaw, high fives from my sons, a hug from my wife, and words of encouragement from my friends and family of faith.

In Scripture it is written that, in the end, "faith, hope, and love abide, these three; and the greatest of these is love" (1 Cor 13:13).

Will trade husband for shoes

"So do not be afraid; you are of more value than many sparrows."

Matthew 10:31

The sign was prominently displayed in the window of the shoe store: "Will trade husband for shoes." My first thought was what a witty advertisement. It certainly grabbed my attention. Then, as I followed my wife into the store I began to ponder. If Sharon decided to take the offer to trade me for shoes, how many pairs of shoes would I be worth? I hoped that I would be worth at least one pair! Maybe I would be worth five pairs… even more; or perhaps that is just wishful thinking on my part.

The fact is that I prefer more certainty in my life than I was feeling in that shoe store. Fortunately, when I walk into the house of God, I do not encounter signs that I might be traded away by God for a better deal. Without hesitation God promised, "And you shall be my people, / and I will be your God" (Jer 30:22). In Matthew, Jesus says, "I am with you always, to the end of the age" (Matt 28:20). There is no hint of uncertainty in God's promise that we belong to God for eternity.

Sharon told me that she would never trade me for a pair of shoes. It briefly occurred to me to ask if she would give me up for more than one pair, but I decided that there is wisdom in not belaboring the point. Instead, I turned to Matthew 10:31 and read the words of Jesus: "So do not be afraid, you are of more value than many sparrows." In Matthew 5:13, I read, "You are the salt of the earth."

I have decided to stay away from ladies' shoe stores for a while and spend more time contemplating sparrows and salt. You might want to try it!

A **complete** picture

"Death will be no more; / mourning and crying and pain will be no more, / for the first things have passed away."

Revelation 21:4

The relatively new U-Haul truck was driving rather smoothly as I left Dallas, headed for Lubbock. Having signed a two-year lease on a house for my daughter, Erin, and her roommate, I figured that this could be the next-to-last college moving day in which I would be involved. After helping five children with college moves, I savored this thought.

I looked at the side view mirror to see if it was clear to make a lane change. I saw a car about seventy-five yards behind me. I turned on the blinker and began moving over to the lane for slower traffic. At that very moment, I heard the loud honk of a car horn. A dark-colored sedan was moving toward the shoulder to avoid getting hit by me. I jerked the truck back into my lane and took a deep breath. It had been a close call.

After my heart stopped racing, I looked at the side mirror to determine how I could have missed seeing the car next to me. I found the answer at the bottom of the side view mirror. There was a small, round mirror attached to the bottom of the bigger and longer mirror. The larger mirror is for seeing traffic coming up behind the large U-Haul truck. The smaller mirror reveals vehicles right next to the truck. I had not looked at the smaller mirror before making the lane change. So I did not have a complete picture of the traffic situation before I attempted to change lanes. Not having a complete picture could have led to tragedy.

In worship one summer, we studied the book of Revelation. One insight I gained from the sermon series was that we (pastors and teachers) fail, more often than not, to communicate the complete picture of this book. Many parishioners view Revelation as a book dedicated solely to the final judgment of humankind, fraught with descriptions of grotesque beasts, hellfire, and destruction. Many believe that the primary goal of the writer is to frighten the reader into becoming a Christian believer.

However, a complete view of the intent of Revelation requires understanding that the early Christians were already overwhelmed with fear of persecution for their beliefs by the Roman authorities. The author is attempting to give hope and assurance to a terrified faith community that the power of the Lord God Almighty is greater than the evil perpetrated by the Roman authorities. Faith is stronger than fear. In the end God, not evil, will win. John of Patmos writes:

> And I heard a loud voice from the throne saying,
> "See, the home of God is among mortals.

He will dwell with them;
they will be his people,
and God himself will be with them;
he will wipe every tear from their eyes.
Death will be no more;
mourning and crying and pain will be no more,
for the first things have passed away."
Revelation 21:3-4

Let us pray for God to guide us away from the tragedy of a distorted picture of God's Word for our lives; instead, by grace, may we grasp a more complete view of God's saving Word and presence.

Undignified

"Lord, when was it that we saw you... a stranger... and did not take care of you?"

Matthew 25:44

On a return flight to Dallas, a member of our church family was reflecting on the meaning of the word "undignified" as it applied to her faith journey. Praying as she peered out the window of the airplane, she was surprised that she could so clearly see the steeple of St. Andrew as the aircraft passed over Plano.

Upon landing around 6:30 p.m., she walked to the loading area to catch the shuttle to the remote parking lot. Due to frequent business trips, she knew the driver and spoke to him as she boarded the bus. To her amazement, there was only one other passenger on the shuttle that evening. A man talking on a cell phone sat a few seats away from her. She heard him say to the person on the other end of the phone, "All we know right now is that there is no brain damage." He thanked the person for calling and turned off his phone. Then he began to cry.

She looked over at him and said, "I have no idea what is going on in your life. I don't need to know, but I am praying for you right now. Is that all right?"

The stranger responded, "Yes, please."

This ambassador of Christ then moved next to him, put her hand on his back, and asked, "Can you tell me what you would like me to pray for?"

Between deep sobs he explained, "Please pray for my six-year-old son who was hit by a car. He has been Care-Flighted to the hospital. His name is Logan." She prayed for Logan, his father, and the doctors who were caring for his son.

This church member then asked the bus driver to take the father to his car first. She even offered to drive him to the hospital where his son had been taken. The father told her that he could make it. Then, he left with these words: "I don't know what to say. But thank you so much."

As the father drove away, the bus driver turned and declared, "That is the most unbelievable thing that I have ever seen!"

Some might call what took place on the shuttle that evening presumptuous and even a little undignified. Others would see this as a bold witness of faith. I believe that the words and actions of this member of our St. Andrew family were a powerful testimony to the amazing grace of God at work through those who believe. King David himself proclaimed, "I will celebrate before the Lord. I will become even more undignified than this [for the Lord's sake]" (2 Sam 6:21c-22a NIV).

I choose **her** for my team

"(God) knows the secrets of the heart."

Psalm 44:21

Sandlot football was all the rage in Magnolia, Arkansas, where we had recently moved due to my father's new job. I was comfortable as an eighth grader and as the new kid on the block jumping into a pickup football game no matter the age or the abilities of the guys who were playing.

I also made a point to bring my fifth-grade sister Sara with me when looking for a game. When the time came to select our teams, Sara was always my first choice. You should have seen some of the looks of disbelief when I chose my sister for my sandlot football team over other players. However, their bewilderment quickly turned to astonishment as she took the handoff and ran like the wind with the football, darting with the quickness of a water bug, into the opponent's end zone.

You know, we all too often spend a lot of time and effort judging people on the basis of their appearance, gender, or the color of their skin. We fail to take into account the character of a person or the nature of their God-given gifts. That was always a mistake when it came to underestimating the character and talent of my little sister.

Is there someone created by the Lord God whom you might be dismissing due to underestimating the strength of their character and the nature of their God-given gifts? Will you make room on your team?

Bottles of milk left on a stoop

"The rendering of this ministry not only supplies the needs of the saints but also overflows with many thanksgivings to God."

2 Corinthians 9:12

Edythe Weiner was a founding member of St. Andrew. I will remember her as one of the most generous and compassionate persons I have ever known. When our church needed help in those early years, Edythe was one of the first to volunteer. She served as our very first Sunday school superintendent. She was legendary for greeting the children arriving for Sunday school with a smile and outstretched arms saying, "How about a hug today?" Edythe and Rev. Charles Stokes founded the senior group in our church called PALS (People with Active Lifestyles). Clearly, Edythe had an exceptional passion to serve, which distinguished her from all the rest of us.

One day over lunch, I gained some insight into how Edythe came to have such a generous servant's heart. She talked about the strong faith of her parents, especially the faith of her father, Abram. Abram owned and operated a dairy farm in Windber, Pennsylvania. During the Great Depression, Edythe said that her family struggled to survive, just like thousands of other families who lived in the

Windber area. However, when she would go with her father into town to deliver bottles of fresh milk, he would place milk on the stoop of the homes of all his customers, whether or not they could pay him. When told by a family that they could no longer afford the milk, he would simply say that, in time, they would be back on their feet. They could pay him then.

Many years later, after many of his customers had passed away and their children were grown with families of their own, Edythe's father died. As Edythe stood in the receiving line after the funeral service, person after person began handing her envelopes. In the envelopes were notes of gratitude for her father's compassion during the Depression along with the money the families owed him for the life-saving milk he had continued to deliver. The children who drank the milk he left on the stoop were thanking Edythe for her father's Christlike generosity.

I then realized the faith of Edythe's father and his generous lifestyle had been passed down to Edythe. Edythe then passed down the gift of generosity to her children, grandchildren, and to her church family. What legacy will you leave to your children, grandchildren, friends, and family?

The gift of persistence

"I press on... because Christ Jesus has made me his own."

Philippians 3:12

Our daughter, Erin, was five years old when she asked her mother if she could set up a lemonade stand on the street corner. Sharon told her no because she was tired and was going to her bedroom to take a nap. So, with the lemonade stand no longer an option, Erin decided to empty the refrigerator of sodas, water, and juice boxes. She loaded the drinks into her brother's red wagon and went door to door selling the contents of our refrigerator to the neighbors. When her mom awoke from her nap, she found that the refrigerator was emptied of drinks and that the contents were selling like hotcakes at half the original purchase price.

Erin's mom now describes her daughter's interpretation of the word "no" as meaning "not yet." Clearly, Erin has been given, by the Lord God Almighty himself, the gift of persistence, which she has exercised over and over again since she was five years of age.

It seems, however, that the Lord is not only the source of this unique characteristic, but also embodies the very definition of the word "persistence". After the fall of humankind in the Garden of Eden that led to estrangement from God, the Lord God Almighty embarked on a mission to bring humankind back into a relationship with God. He sent Abraham, Moses, judges, kings, and prophets to accomplish this mission; time and time again, humankind said no. God heard no only as not yet. Finally, God sent his only Son, "so that everyone who believes in him may not perish but may have eternal life" (John 3:16). We now have an everlasting relationship with God through Christ.

Despite what we parents might think of the persistence our children display, in God's eyes this trait was an essential ingredient in the ultimate salvation of humankind through the death and resurrection of God's Son, Jesus Christ. Let us celebrate the persistence of followers of Christ in using time, spiritual gifts, financial resources, and service to fulfill God's mission on earth. Let's not take no for an answer. If we must, we can simply declare "Not yet!" By God's grace and in God's time, we will find an alternate path to accomplish the Lord's purpose.

Dancing angels

"Then turning to the disciples, Jesus said to them privately, 'Blessed are the eyes that see what you see!'"

Luke 10:23

While sitting on a balcony at a friend's lakehouse in East Texas, I listened to the rustling leaves as the wind whipped through the trees. The dead leaves were being tossed to and fro as they began their descent from the branches toward the ground below. Many of the falling leaves looked as if they were dancing in mid-air; they were captured by multiple gusts of wind.

Now we may see falling leaves as an unwelcome sign of the arrival of winter accompanied by the never-ending battle to rake and bag the leaves. Falling leaves can mark an end to a very colorful season, making way for the barren and somber hues of winter. Yet, for some, falling leaves are like dancing angels. These waltzing angels announce the coming birth of the Light of the World and the Prince of Peace, the Christ child.

I pray for eyes that can see dancing angels in falling, brown, dead leaves. I pray for the vision to see new beginnings in the endings of life. I pray that I can discover joy in life events that seem void of color. I pray that you and I will make room in our lives for sightings of dancing.

Leading by faith

"The angel said to them, "Do not be afraid; for see—I am bringing you good news of great joy for all the people: to you is born this day in the city of David a Savior, who is the Messiah, the Lord."

Luke 2:10-11

I was offensive coordinator for our Pythons sixth grade PSA football team and our head coach, who was one of the dads, happened to be a retired Dallas Cowboys football player. For our first game, I put some significant pressure on myself to call the right plays in order to march down the field (like the Dallas Cowboys) and score against our opponents. Even though I had played running back for the mighty Red Panthers of Magnolia High School, I was having no success.

My son, Will, who was the quarterback of the Pythons, eventually came up to me and said, "Dad, please let me call the plays. I know we can score a touchdown against this team." I skeptically consented, "All right, one play." The result was that we scored a touchdown on that one play. Then, more touchdowns followed the more I trusted my son to lead the offense.

A lesson that I learned that day was that we have a

choice to either lead by faith or lead by fear. My son, Will, modeled leading by faith as he exhibited confidence in the God-given abilities of his teammates. Will's proclivity toward fearlessness continues to this day as he now serves the Lord in full-time Christian ministry as an ordained United Methodist minister. Leading by faith doesn't necessarily lead to touchdowns or to worldly treasures; but faithful living does lead us away from fear and toward a wellness in our soul through service to God and others.

Asking for help

"So I say to you, Ask, and it will be given you; search, and you will find; knock, and the door will be opened for you. For everyone who asks receives, and everyone who searches finds, and for everyone who knocks, the door will be opened."

Luke 11:9-10

One Sunday evening, a mom, who is also a professional therapist, gathered her children to talk to them about the tragedy at Sandy Hook Elementary School in Newtown, Connecticut. She shared with her preschool children that the man who broke into the school had a disease in his brain. Her daughter thought about this for a minute. Then she responded, "Momma, he should have come to see you. You would have made him better, and he would not have done those terrible things." Out of the mouth of a child came words of wisdom that might help us all.

That preschooler recognized that, when you are not thinking right or feeling right, it is a good idea to ask someone for help. Many of us find ourselves in a bad place but fail to reach out for a helping hand in our time of need. Why is this so? I believe that there are times we do not see our need for help. On other occasions, we decide to deal with our issues on our own. Or we might feel too embarrassed to ask for assistance. Sometimes, we are not sure where to turn for help, so we put it off indefinitely.

Jesus teaches, "Ask, and it will be given you; search, and you will find; knock, and the door will be opened for you. For everyone who asks receives, and everyone who searches finds, and for everyone who knocks, the door will be opened" (Luke 11:9-10). Maybe it is the right time to take the advice of a child: Ask for help in our time of need or allow someone else to lead us to help when we fail to see our need for it.

Jesus says, "[F]or it is to such as these [children] that the kingdom of heaven belongs" (Matt 19:14). In other words, children often seem to have a more direct line to divine truth than the rest of us.

An unlikely connection

"He ran ahead and climbed a sycamore tree to see [Jesus], because he was going to pass that way."

Luke 19:4

I was headed to Cowboys Stadium with my sons, Stephen, John, and their friend Judd, to watch a Cotton Bowl game between Oklahoma and Texas A&M. There was a tent pitched just outside the entrance that sheltered both a replica of the Heisman Trophy and a gentleman standing next to it in a Sooners jersey. I took the opportunity to introduce myself to Billy Sims. He was the 1978 Heisman Trophy winner and later an All-Pro running back for the Detroit Lions. He was signing autographs.

I asked him to sign my Cotton Bowl ticket and then I mentioned that I had watched him play a high school football game in Hooks, Texas. His Hooks High School team played my alma mater, the "Mighty Red Panthers" of Magnolia High School. I recounted that he scored a touchdown every time he touched the football. Surprisingly, he remembered almost every detail of that game. After a prolonged conversation, he shook my hand and said, "Thank you for the memories." I left energized by the time we spent together and glad that I had taken the initiative, at the urging of my sons and their friend, to make the connection.

The moment made me wonder: how many times do we bypass the opportunity to connect with people around us? The Lord gives us stories, like that of Zacchaeus in the Gospel of Luke, to remind us that connecting with others can significantly change our lives. Let us not be shy about making a connection with another. We might be surprised at the good things that could happen.

Friends make a difference

"Then some people came, bringing to [Jesus] a paralyzed man, carried by four of them."

Mark 2:3

We rushed to the hospital with our firstborn on the way. I was mentally rehearsing the coaching I was trained to provide my wife during labor, when the doctor came out to tell me that our son was breech. Instead of having the opportunity to be in the delivery room for the birth of my first child, I had to remain in the waiting area. I tried to choke back the feelings of disappointment that I would not be present for the delivery. In addition, I had a growing fear that this unexpected development could put my wife and child in harm's way. Few times in my life have I felt so utterly alone and helpless.

While at my lowest point, I was completely surprised when my friend Jim walked into the waiting room. Somehow he had heard that I had taken my wife to the hospital. He came by to check on us. I was never so glad to see a familiar face. A father himself, Jim reassured me that everything would be all right, and then he prayed with me. Because of his faith and compassion, the feelings of loneliness and helplessness vanished. My thoughts turned instead to the pure joy of becoming a father.

Friends are like that, aren't they? They can bring the light of hope into our darkest hours. That is what took place in the story of the healing of the paralyzed man recorded in the Gospel of Mark 2:1-12. Four of the paralyzed man's friends carried him to Jesus to be healed because they saw the isolation and loneliness he experienced due to his inability to walk. We are told that, because of the faith of his friends, not only was the man able to walk again, his heart was also healed when Jesus forgave his sins. Because of the faith of his four friends, the paralyzed man was made well.

The faith, prayers, and presence of friends make a difference. Therefore, hold onto your friends with both hands. Better yet, be a friend to someone else!

What's in a name?

"'[A]nd they shall name him Emmanuel,' which means, 'God is with us.'"

Matthew 1:23

My youngest son, Will, and his wife, Amanda, asked me to come up with a list of family names from which they might choose the name of their daughter, who was to be born around New Year's Day. Between my father, who was one of twelve children, and my mother, who was one of four, I had plenty of names from which they could choose. A few of their choices included Era Lee, Bessie Mae, Emogene, Charlene, Idy Mae, and Maude.

They chose Emogene.

Aunt Emogene had a larger than life God-given personality. She would light up a room with her smile, laughter, and stories. My granddaughter Emogene likewise lights up a room with her God-given energetic personality, continual dialogue, and radiant smile. I have always believed that there is something in a name that helps to shape and determine the personality of the one who carries that name. That is certainly the case with Emogene.

The names of my other two likewise amazing granddaughters, Angel and Joy, have served to not only shape their persona but daily remind us and them of who they are and whose they are. What comfort and assurance I find in being reminded each time I call their names that God, through our Lord, Emmanuel, is with all three of them to guide and watch over them always.

What love looks like

"[Love] always protects, always trusts, always hopes, always perseveres."

1 Corinthians 13:7 NIV

Some time ago, Dan, the father of the bride, walked his only daughter, Katy, down the center aisle of our Sanctuary. Over the years, hundreds of fathers have escorted their daughters down this aisle to present them to their future husbands. But what transpired this time was different from all the other weddings I have witnessed over my thirty-plus years in ministry.

Dan had suffered a stroke that cost him the use of his right leg. Now, you need to know that the center aisle in our Sanctuary is one of the longest in the Dallas/Fort Worth area. It also slopes significantly downward as you walk toward the altar. Therefore, it can be somewhat challenging (even if you have two, strong, healthy legs) to make it from the back of the Sanctuary to the altar on your daughter's wedding day, without a misstep. However, Dan decided that his stroke, along with his ensuing disability, would not prevent him from walking his daughter down the aisle on her special day.

Once a week for two months, Dan came to the church with his physical therapist to prepare to attempt the improbable for his daughter. Then, on the evening of the ceremony, as the wedding march was played and the doors to the Sanctuary were flung open, there stood both Dan and Katy. With Katy's arm laced through her father's arm, and Dan's hands firmly gripping his walker, they made their way down the aisle of the Sanctuary of St. Andrew United Methodist Church. He used the strength of his left leg and hip to take one step and then another. Firmly planted in front of the altar, he responded to the question posed by the minister: "Who presents this woman to be married to this man?" Dan's answer: "With great joy, her mother and I do!"

Amidst freely flowing tears, a brief silence was broken by a standing ovation from the wedding guests!

What does love look like? Love looks like a father who overcame a tremendous obstacle to be able to walk his daughter down the aisle on her wedding day.

What does love look like? Love looks like a Heavenly Father who overcame tremendous obstacles to walk with us down a path of faith that leads us into the light of God's amazing grace.

Thank you, Dan, for opening our eyes to see and our hearts to be touched by selfless love that is truly divine!

Both a bad day and a good day

"Then God said, 'Let there be light';

and there was light."

Genesis 1:3

My niece Callie went on her church's confirmation retreat. Her mother asked her about the day of the traditional candlelight worship service. Callie replied, "It was both a good day and a bad day." She proceeded to explain that her candle would not light at the worship service. That was the bad part of the day. The good part of the day was that everybody in her confirmation group tried to help her light her candle. Even though none of her classmates were able to get the candle lit, the fact that they all tried to help her transformed what she felt was a bad day into a good day.

What came to mind as I heard Callie's comment is how our faith in the grace and eternal hope of Christ has a way of turning our bad days into good days, or at least better days than we expect. My son John and I visited with a good friend who had just been placed in hospice care. Knowing that our friend was very sick and approaching the end of his life, John and I had a difficult time preparing ourselves emotionally for the visit. However, once we got there, we encountered more joy than sadness as we talked about the good times we all shared over the years. There were water volleyball games in the backyard of our friend's home and the family gatherings at church where we would catch up on our activities during the week. What looked to be a bad day, coming face-to-face with the imminent loss of a good friend, became a good day as we celebrated wonderful memories and the gift of the life we had shared.

After hearing about the explosions near the finish line of the Boston Marathon, my first responses were disbelief, shock, horror, and anger. I did not want to watch the news for fear that everything reported would simply confirm that this would go down as one of the worst days in the history of our nation. However, I finally gave in and turned on the television. What I saw and heard surprised me. I saw a photograph of Martin Richard, an eight-year-old boy who was killed by this inexcusable act of terror, holding up a sign that he had made at school that read "No More Hurting People, Peace." I thought, out of the mouth of a child had come a truth that all the world must embrace. This was followed by the story of a man, Carlos, who had lost two sons over the past few years, one to war and then another to suicide. He was at the finish line, handing out American flags to runners. When the explosions occurred, instead of running away, he ran toward the devastation, helping to save the life of a young man who had lost his legs in the blast.

I believe that bad days become good days when we can see the grace of God at work in the world, or when we become instruments of that grace, like Callie's confirmation friends, my friend in hospice, my son John, Martin Richards, and Carlos. God's grace is so amazing that the light of that grace can shine on even the darkest days of our lives. Thanks be to God.

The gift of memory

"Then he took a loaf of bread, and when he had given thanks, he broke it and gave it to them, saying, 'This is my body, which is given for you. Do this in remembrance of me.'"

Luke 22:19

After my sister Barbara traveled to Gurdon, Arkansas, to visit relatives, she reported that lightning had struck our Grandmother Stephens' old home place. The second story of the house was virtually destroyed by fire. My sister was told that her old home would probably be torn down.

Upon hearing this news, a great sorrow came over me. However, the sadness lifted as I began recalling my childhood memories of Grandmother's Gurdon home. I remember repeatedly walking up and down the stairs that led to the second floor so I could hear the old wooden steps creak under my feet. Rummaging through the upstairs attic of the house one summer, I discovered old newspapers from World War I and World War II. I was ecstatic when Grandmother gave me permission to take the papers to school for show and tell.

The first floor was the living area where we sat for hours listening to Grandmother play, by ear, hymns and popular songs of the day on her baby grand piano. Then, there was the large front porch where my grandmother and I would sit in the porch swing, visiting about all sorts of things that I never seemed able to talk about with anyone but her.

After receiving news about the destruction of the old home, remembering those special times was healing for me. When we participate in the Lord's Supper, we are given the gift of remembering. As we partake of the bread, representing the body of Christ broken for us; and drink from the cup, representing the blood of Christ shed for us; we remember that "God so loved the world that he gave his only Son, so that everyone who believes in him may not perish but may have eternal life" (John 3:16). This is a memory that brings healing and hope to our lives. What a wonderful gift!

A high-flying Father's Day present

"Trust in the Lord with all your heart, / and do not rely on your own insight."

Proverbs 3:5

My oldest son, Stephen, bought me an airline ticket for Father's Day so that I could fly to Denver to visit him. He also rented a single prop airplane to fly me from the Boulder Airport to the Greeley Airport for a Father's Day breakfast. A good friend asked me if I was nervous, knowing that Stephen had only recently received his pilot's license and that he had flown a very limited number of trips with passengers. My answer, "I was not nervous at all." My trust in his ability is a product of my personal experience and knowledge of my son.

As my firstborn, he is extremely responsible and trustworthy. He has the gift of attention to detail, which is a wonderful trait to have when running through a preflight checklist. He is not one to take unnecessary risks when it comes to assessing weather conditions suitable for flying. He told me ahead of time that, if the wind conditions were not just right, he would not be comfortable taking me up. He would rather reschedule for another time than risk having an accident.

I imagine that many of you, after reading my assessment of Stephen's capabilities as a pilot, might be willing to fly with him, even though he is a newly trained pilot. If we can find a way to trust a novice pilot with our lives, why is it that we have so much difficulty placing our lives in the hands of the Lord God Almighty?

Is it because we believe the Lord hasn't had sufficient life skills training? No; God has been studying humankind ever since first breathing the breath of life into the first human being.

Is our lack of ability to place our complete faith in the Lord due to anything God has done to betray our trust? I suggest this has not happened either; nor will it happen. As the psalmist declares: "The Lord is my shepherd, I shall not want. /... / Surely goodness and mercy shall follow me / all the days of my life, and I shall dwell in the house of the Lord / my whole life long" (Psalm 23:1,6).

Is our lack of trust in God primarily due to our lack of ability to let go of control over our lives, to let God be our pilot (or shepherd) who helps us to navigate through life? I believe this is our primary block to flying high with God. We are unwilling to let go of the steering mechanism. I believe that our only hope in becoming more trusting is by God's grace and our willingness to grow in the knowledge and love of God. We must desire to know the Lord more intimately, as a parent knows a child. We must make it a priority to be in worship each Sunday. We need to set aside time to study holy scripture, to be a part of a connection group where we can discuss the ways God is working in our daily lives, to serve the Lord by serving others, and to give of our time and financial resources to make trusting disciples of Jesus Christ. By simply practicing the presence of God through observing the spiritual disciplines, we can come to experience, know, and love God more fully. The fruit of this pathway to the Divine is that we come to trust the Lord more.

Do you trust the Lord enough to put your life in the Lord's hand? If so, I guarantee that you will fly higher than you have ever flown before; the view from the Lord's heavenly vantage point is breathtaking!

An undivided heart

"Teach me your way, O Lord, / that I may walk in your truth; / give me an undivided heart to revere your name."

Psalm 86:11

My second-grade teacher began lining us up in front of the class based on our score on the Weekly Reader quiz. I was placed third from the last. My humiliation was so great that I made up my mind then and there that I would never again be embarrassed by poor grades. Studying became my number one priority.

Academic success was my primary motivation entering college, during which time I regularly skipped church to do homework. However, I would simultaneously tell others that my love for the Lord was leading me to consider seminary and the ordained ministry. While in college, I remember my father inviting me to an event where he would be receiving a prestigious honor in his chosen field of public school education. I deeply loved and respected my father. However, I turned down his invitation because I had a big test the next day. I stayed and studied for the test. I will always regret having missed my father's special day.

Over time, I began to realize the fear of failure that filled a large portion of my heart was negatively affecting my relationships with God, family, and friends. My preoccupation with academic success was taking priority over my devotion to the most significant people in my life. Likewise, the joy that those relationships brought was also fading away.

My heart was divided. Part of me was living out of fear of failure, which led to my obsession with academic success. Success had become an idol that I worshiped; yet it brought no lasting satisfaction, only loneliness and isolation. At the same time, another part of me was living out of faith in a God who offered a life of faith, hope, love, and joy.

Only through the grace of God, through faith, did I begin to see the unhealthy nature of a divided heart, devoted to serving both human-made idols and the Lord God Almighty as revealed in Jesus Christ. When confronted by my human frailty that results in idol worship, I have found that the road to recovery of spiritual health and wholeness is paved with the power of prayer. That's why I am drawn to the Psalms, which gives us words to pray in our time of need (see Psalm 86).

Through prayer, we also discover the power of the Lord to "gather you from… where you have been scattered…. I will give [you] one heart, and put a new spirit within [you]" (Ezek 11:17-20). Consider putting God first through prayer in your living and in your giving. The fruit of such a commitment is the divine blessing of an undivided heart.

The undoing of good works

"I am making all things new."

Revelation 21:5

The sisters, ages two and three, were assigned the role of flower girls for the wedding. On cue, the two siblings, wearing their dainty white dresses, each carrying a basket full of flower petals, began their procession down the long center aisle of the Sanctuary. All eyes were on them, including mine, as they slowly (very slowly) made their way down the aisle. The older sister was laser-focused on her role. Every two steps she took, she would stop to drop a single flower petal. Then, she would proceed to take another two steps, stop, and drop another.

However, her two-year-old sister had a different agenda. Clearly for her, littering was a big issue and dropping flower petals on the floor and not picking them up was unacceptable. So, during the processional, the younger sister trailed behind her older sister a couple of steps, picking up each flower petal that her sibling dropped in the aisle. She then put the dropped petal into her own basket. When the sisters arrived at the front of the church, the aisle was clear of any unsightly debris (flower petals in this case) due to the fastidiousness of a two-year-old.

I did not see the reaction of the older sister when she

realized that her effort to faithfully carry out her role of flower girl was undone by her little sister. However, I do know how it feels to have your good work undone by circumstances beyond your control. Jesus, himself, invested three years of effort in proclaiming the good news of the gospel; yet a few people, who had an entirely different agenda, attempted to undo all that he had accomplished. The good news is that God took the seeds (the good works) that were planted by his Only Begotten Son in the hearts and minds of his followers and nurtured them until the work that was undone began to be accomplished through them.

A warm blanket for the Christ child

"And the King will answer them, 'Truly I tell you, just as you did it to one of the least of these who are members of my family, you did it to me.'"

Matthew 25:40

Project Hope is a ministry offered by The Storehouse of Collin County, founded and supported by St. Andrew to help families or individuals break out of the cycle of poverty. One of our Project Hope clients shared that she hoped to work as a seamstress one day. Our Project Hope coaches encouraged her to pursue a job in her field, but several roadblocks deterred her progress. The coaches and the client began to pray about how she might move forward with her dream of one day becoming a seamstress.

While turning to the Lord in prayer, the amazing grace of God became evident. Henny, a first-time visitor to St. Andrew, came to church on a Sunday we were highlighting Project Hope. She approached a Project Hope volunteer to say that she did not know how she might be of assistance, but she felt drawn to the program. Henny further explained that she was a fashion designer/accomplished seamstress by trade and had hosted sewing classes for less fortunate women and children. A few weeks later, a Project Hope Advisory Board member was approached by someone who explained that they had been given two sewing machines to donate but was not sure what agency might be able to use them. The donation was accepted and Henny, along with the Project Hope client, began a weekly sewing class at St. Andrew, open to the entire community.

Henny (who is now a member of the church) traveled to Afghanistan to help empower women by beginning a vocational program. While there, she learned that hundreds of thousands of refugees returning to their homeland were forced to live in tents on the outskirts of Kabul. They barely survived; the previous winter, hundreds of people (including many children) died from the cold. Henny felt a passion to respond. She decided to use reams of fabric donated to the sewing class to make blankets to send to the refugees. Over the course of three months, the women in the Project Hope sewing class created more than two hundred blankets to send to Afghanistan.

This touching story reminds me of Jesus' words from the Gospel of Matthew. Prayer moves us to become givers of blankets that provide physical and spiritual warmth to those in need. I wonder if the shepherds who visited the manger might have covered the Christ child with a woolen blanket to keep him warm. Each time we provide warmth and comfort to someone in need, scripture teaches us that we are providing for the needs of Christ. What will the blanket look like that you will offer someone in need in the name of Christ?

Taking home the leftovers

"You give them something to eat."

Mark 6:37

A day trip to visit my Grandmother Stephens meant a delicious home-cooked meal. There was always more food placed in front of us than we could ever eat in one sitting. So we could count on going home with leftovers that would feed our family of five for at least a week. No one else ever came close to providing food for our family the way Grandmother Stephens did. It was her way of saying how much she loved us.

Over two thousand years ago, a trip to hear Jesus teach meant feasting on a spiritual meal. However, one extraordinary day, five thousand visitors (with the women and children the number was closer to twenty thousand) were not only spiritually fed, but also had the miraculous experience of being physically nourished by Jesus.

It was late in the day when the disciples pointed out to the Teacher that the people who were gathered around him had not eaten. They wanted Jesus to dismiss the crowd in order that they might go into the surrounding countryside to find something to eat. Instead, Jesus told his disciples to provide food for them. The disciples brought five loaves and two fish to Jesus. Jesus looked up to heaven, gave thanks, and broke the bread. Then he gave his disciples the five loaves and two fish to distribute to the multitude.

Mark tells us, "And all ate and were filled" (Mark 6:42). After the meal, the disciples gathered up twelve baskets of leftovers. I imagine that, like Grandmother Stephens did for us, Jesus gave the crowd the leftovers to take home to eat during the week. This was simply another way for Jesus to communicate to the thousands gathered that day the depth and breadth of God's love for them. This miracle revealed to them that the Lord God could be trusted to provide for all their needs, just as God provided spiritual food and manna for the Hebrews on their journey through the wilderness.

A hammer gone astray

"Forgive us for the ways we have wronged you, /

just as we also forgive those who have wronged us."

Matthew 6:12 CEB

Our youth group was on a mission trip to repair homes in an area of Atlanta, Georgia, hit by urban blight. We were wrapping up a roof repair project the afternoon of our last day, when one of our youth requested a hammer to finish pounding in the final few roofing nails. Instead of climbing up the ladder to hand the hammer to the conscientious roofer, the youthful respondent decided to throw it to her fellow volunteer.

She first practiced an underhanded toss; but, for some reason, she changed her mind and threw overhanded. Flying through the air like a tomahawk, the hammer had insufficient arch to reach the roof. Instead, the hammer went straight through the bedroom window. Even worse, the owner was resting on her bed when the hammer came crashing through the glass. Thankfully, the woman was not hurt; but the psyche of the hammer thrower was damaged. The intention to be helpful was pure; however, the outcome of the effort was not only unhelpful but harmful.

The road we travel regarding our significant relationships is paved with good intentions. Yet, all too often, our good intentions to be helpful result in doing harm rather than good. That is why a key ingredient to healthy relationships is forgiveness. Sometimes we need to ask for forgiveness. At other times, we are called on to forgive another person or even to forgive ourselves.

Forgiveness won out in Atlanta. My prayer is that forgiveness will have the last word in your relationships as well.

Sealed with a kiss

"And if I… do not have love, I am nothing."

1 Corinthians 13:2

Sharon and I put a lot of thought and prayer into planning for our wedding day. We asked Sharon's seven-year-old daughter Erin to serve as the flower girl. Erin was to stand with us at the altar during the ceremony and throw the flower petals after I kissed her mom. Of course, what I had in mind was that Erin would shower us with the petals at the end of the service when I responded to the minister's declaration: "You may kiss your bride."

The ceremony began. I was totally captivated by Sharon's radiance and beauty. As a matter of fact, I was so taken with her that, during a pause between our vows, I could not help myself. I leaned over and kissed her on the cheek. Erin noticed.

In keeping with the instructions I had given, Erin grabbed a huge handful of petals and threw them high in the air. The minister was startled and flustered by the sudden interruption in the order of service. Sharon and I continued to look at each other and smile. Against the traditional script, I kissed her again, and again. The flowers floated down around us.

Now, years later, I find myself still captivated by Sharon's radiant beauty. Spontaneously, I will lean forward and give her a kiss. We might be at home, at a movie, in the grocery store, or at church. We might be visiting with friends over a meal, or I might be serving her Communion in worship when I will lean over and give her a kiss. (I usually make it a point to explain to the next person in line for Communion that I don't kiss everyone that comes forward for Communion, only my wife.)

These moments always take me back to our wedding day when I vowed that "I, Robert, take you Sharon… to love and to cherish until death do us part." I sealed that vow with a kiss before God, friends, and family. As a matter of fact, I sealed it with more than one kiss that day, and I continue to seal it again and again with additional kisses that communicate my promise to love and cherish her.

God chose to seal God's love for us with a rainbow and then a cross. What action are you willing to take to seal your love for our Lord and for the people God has placed in your life?

The **gift** of life

"I give you a new commandment, that you love one another. Just as I have loved you, you also should love one another."

John 13: 34

One Sunday morning several years ago a heart-transplant recipient stood up in one of our St. Andrew worship services and thanked the Lord for the person whose donated heart made it possible for him to be alive. The organ donor was Gary Arnold. Gary and his family were members of St. Andrew at the time of his fatal accident. In the midst of their sorrow, Gary's family honored his wishes to be an organ donor, thus saving a life.

I recently spoke at John Hamilton's memorial service held in our Sanctuary which John, as chair of the St. Andrew Building Committee, helped to build. At that service I was able to announce that John's family had honored his wishes to have his body given to medical science for research with the hope of developing a cure for the cancer that took his life.

"And now faith, hope, and love abide, these three; and the greatest of these is love."

1 Cor 13:13

What are you willing to give in order that another might live? I am pondering my answer.

They will call the child— God with Us

"'And they shall name him Emmanuel,'

which means, 'God is with us.'"

Matthew 1:23

This scripture (found in both Isa 7:14 and Matt 1:23) came to mind when I received the following story from a member of our medical team staff at the medical clinic the St. Andrew family helped to establish for the Cabécars in Jabuy, Costa Rica:

> Wednesday morning, June 4, a young man arrived at the clinic and asked if we could go get his pregnant wife. They were coming to Jabuy from their home in Canabre, which is a three-hour walk. She had stopped along the way, unable to go any further because of contractions. The husband and I took off in the jeep to pick her up. When we found her, she had already given birth to their baby daughter. The mother was alone, off the side of the road, hidden in the jungle.
>
> We helped the mother and baby into the jeep and sped toward the clinic. The doctor and nurse checked and cleaned the baby, cut/clamped

> the umbilical cord, and swaddled her in a new, clean blanket. Upon examining the baby, they found that she was doing well. The mother was still bleeding from the delivery. So, we all loaded up (baby, mother, father, and the clinic staff) and headed down the mountain. We took them to Valle Clinic, where the doctor and the nurse checked out the mother and baby. They were both in good condition; however, as a precaution, he sent them to the hospital in Limon.
>
> We are thankful for many things—a newborn healthy baby girl, a safe delivery, and a mother who is doing well. Unfortunately, due to the urgency of the situation we did not get anyone's name. But God knows the names and God is keeping account of the baby, her mother, father, and four-year-old sibling who live high in the southeastern mountains in Costa Rica."

In sharing this story with the congregation, I proposed that we refer to this newborn baby girl as "God with us" (which is also the meaning of the name for our clinic, Clínica Emanuel). For indeed, the Lord was with the mother and child on the day of her birth. I thank the Lord God Almighty for the opportunity to be a representative of God's healing to the Cabécar tribe. I find it rather miraculous that, even in a remote jungle in Costa Rica, a grass-lined manger can cradle the hope of new life in Christ.

A **helping** hand

"You shall love the Lord your God with all your heart, and with all your soul, and with all your strength, and with all your mind; and your neighbor as yourself."

Luke 10:27

Stating the obvious, ice skating rinks are not plentiful in South Arkansas. So when my nine-year-old niece Callie moved with her family from Magnolia, Arkansas, to the Dallas area, ice skating was a new and exciting recreational opportunity. When Callie put on skates, she discovered that ice skating is not as easy as it looks on television. After falling on her backside for the fifth time, she looked up at her mom and dad and frustratingly declared, "You know, it's much easier to fall than it is to get up." Out of the mouth of a child often comes truth worth pondering.

Of course, falling down is a part of living. We fell down a lot as we learned to walk for the first time. As adults, falling down takes on a different form. We fall short of the expectations of others or of our own. I suggest that falling short of expectations is a frequent occurrence for all of us, especially when it comes to following God's will for our lives. Jesus is clear about what God expects from us: "You shall love the Lord your God with all your heart, and with all your soul, and with all your strength, and with all your mind; and your neighbor as yourself" (Luke 10:27). But, as Callie put it, falling down (or falling short) is easy; what's hard is getting back up.

What happened next at the ice rink is significant. With a helping hand and encouragement from her mom and dad, Callie kept getting back up on her skates. Then, after several more failed attempts, she was able to skate on ice for the first time. Likewise, God helps us to succeed in following his will for our lives, extending to us a helping hand called forgiveness. God's forgiveness gives us the opportunity to get back up when we fall short of loving God, others, and self. God then encourages us to try again. God tells us we are, "the salt of the earth… [and] the light of the world" (Matt 5:13-14). So, with God's help, let's stand back up, wipe ourselves off (leave our failures behind), and make another attempt today to follow God's will for us. Getting back up is harder than falling down, but it's well worth the effort.

Faith shapes culture when...

"Do not be conformed to this world, but be transformed by the renewing of your minds, so that you may discern what is the will of God—what is good and acceptable and perfect."

Romans 12:2

Faith shapes culture when people like Emily Mills respond to a calling to free women who are caught in the web of the commercial sex industry. Speaking at the Q Conference (a Christian version of "Ted Talks") held at St. Andrew, Emily indicated that a major contributing factor to women turning to the commercial sex trade is sexual abuse and physical violence suffered at the hands of family members during childhood. She shared that she too had been sexually abused as a child and how her pain had been transformed into purpose.

The gospel of Jesus Christ brought hope and empowerment to Emily's life. Now, Emily shares the love of Christ with women across the country through the ministry she founded, Jesus Said Love. Her mission is to awaken hope and empower change in women's lives that they might find freedom from the trauma of exploitation and trafficking. Her prayer is that God might use her as an instrument of unconditional love that opens the possibility of a new life in Christ for women in the sex trade who have been used and abused.

Emily's personal testimony reminds me that, when we say yes to following Jesus Christ, we are freed to no longer fall prey to the lusts of culture. Instead, we are called to stand with Christ in shaping the culture around us by the power of God's transforming love. In what ways are you and I shaping culture today in the name of Christ?

Decision point

“[N]ot my will but yours be done.”

Luke 22:42

I had the opportunity to travel to the Holy Land with Dr. Scott and Patti Engle, my wife Sharon, and ninety members plus friends of the St. Andrew family. Words alone cannot describe the spiritual and emotional impact of walking in the footsteps of Jesus.

One of the most powerful moments was the visit to the Garden of Gethsemane. While praying where Jesus had prayed, I looked up to see the site where the temple stood in Jesus’ time. I realized that, as Jesus was praying in the garden, he could see Judas leading the soldiers down the Temple Mount to arrest him. Jesus would have been fully aware that torture and crucifixion were awaiting him.

Jesus had a decision to make. He could either flee with his disciples to safety into the wilderness, or he could stay and face an excruciating death. Fear would have taken Jesus down the first path. Instead, Jesus chose the path of faith, which led him to complete the mission of salvation that God, the Father, had given to him, God’s beloved Son.

Every day, each of us is faced with the choice of either listening to the voice of fear or the voice of faith. Our choice will determine if we will serve as God's representatives in helping to build a future with hope. What is your decision?

Peace! Be still!

"Peace! Be still!"

Mark 4:39

We spent the first night of the St. Andrew Holy Land Pilgrimage in Tiberius, on the Sea of Galilee. This was the perfect beginning to our trip, as Jesus spent the first two-and-a-half years of his ministry around the area of Galilee.

Dawn brought a magnificent sunrise with multiple colors reflecting off the mirrorlike sea. While in awe of God's artistry, I pictured Jesus in a fishing boat crossing the calm water with his disciples. An indescribable peace came over me at that moment.

I wondered if the peace that I was experiencing was anything like that experienced by the disciples while on a boat with Jesus on the Sea of Galilee. Remember, Scripture tells us that a furious storm came up. Waves broke over the sides of the boat, threatening to swamp it. The fearful disciples woke Jesus, who was in the stern sleeping, and informed him of the dire circumstances.

> "[Jesus] woke up and rebuked the wind,
> and said to the sea, 'Peace! Be still!'
> Then the wind ceased, and there was a dead calm."
>
> Mark 4:39

The disciples must have been utterly amazed by Jesus' power to calm the storm and, therefore, their fears. I, too, was amazed that, in the stillness of reflection and prayer, Jesus had the power to calm the storm of thoughts, agendas, and feelings within me and give to me the divine gift of peace in the midst of my fears.

My prayer for you today is that in the midst of your personal fears you, too, can see and hear Jesus calling out to the storms that are swirling around inside of you: "Peace! Be still!"

A special gift

"Be kind to one another, tenderhearted, forgiving one another, as God in Christ has forgiven you."

Ephesians 4:32

My barber, Donna, told me about a friend whose daughter recently graduated from nursing school. The daughter is now working with newborns at a prestigious hospital in a large city. While trimming around my ears, Donna casually commented, "My friend knew from the time her daughter was four that she would choose a public service profession like nursing."

Skeptically, I responded, "How is it possible that she knew what her daughter would choose to do with her life at such an early age?" "Well," said Donna,

> When her daughter was four years old, my friend took her to Walmart on a cold winter day. Her daughter was clutching her baby blanket (which she carried everywhere) as they entered the store. However, as they walked through the front door, a mother and her little girl were walking out into the cold, wearing summerlike clothing and no coats. As the mom grabbed a shopping cart, she turned around to notice that her daughter was no longer beside her. Looking around, she caught sight of her

> daughter walking back outside. Looking through the glass door, she then witnessed something that brought a lump to her throat. Her four-year-old daughter tapped the coatless girl on the shoulder. She then handed her own special baby blanket to that girl, turned around, and walked back into the store to join her mom. That was the day the mother knew that God had given her daughter the gift of compassion, which she would one day use to help meet the needs of others.

This story touched my heart. I sat in silence for a moment and simply said, "That is a very special young girl with an amazing gift. I hope that I will have the privilege of meeting your friend's daughter one day." Whether I ever get to meet her, I was reminded that day that compassion is a very special gift. Compassion is a gift that was perfectly embodied in a child born in a stable in Bethlehem. We honor the Christ child each time we open our hearts to receive God's gift of compassion and pass on that gift to others. Let's honor Christ today by looking for ways to compassionately serve the needs of God's children.

Looking a little bit **foolish**

"They offered him gifts of gold, frankincense, and myrrh."

Matthew 2:11

New Year's Day was absolutely an amazing day for the Hasley household. Our daughter-in-law and son, Amanda and Will, gave birth to a 7 lb.15 oz. girl at 2:25 a.m. on January 1, 2016. They named her Emogene after Will's paternal grandfather's sister, Aunt Emogene; and Lee after Will's maternal grandmother. Then, at 2:30 p.m. on that same day, our niece Lauren and her husband Danny gave birth to our new great-nephew, Gavin Edwards.

That night, to celebrate this joyous occasion, I walked out to our front yard (where I could clearly see the stars) to pray. I looked for a star to symbolize the light of God's love that had shined down on our family that day. However, the night sky was cloudy. It took a while for the clouds to break, so I paced back and forth in front of our house in the middle of the night for some time. As I spotted a single star, I began offering up to God a prayer of thanksgiving for the light of God's love with the births of my granddaughter and great-nephew. I prayed that God's love would shine on Emogene and Gavin all of their days, and that I would become an instrument of God's love for them as I assumed my role as a grandfather and great-uncle.

I would guess that neighbors who observed me pacing back and forth in my yard might have wondered what I was doing. They might have been tempted to come over to find out what was troubling me. If that had happened, would I have been brave enough to tell them that I was offering up a prayer to God for the new members of my family? Or would I have been bold enough to ask my neighbor to join me in offering up a New Year's prayer of thanksgiving for someone who was special to them?

The actions of the magi, who followed a star that they believed would lead to a newborn life-transforming King among the Jews (a relatively insignificant powerless people under Roman rule), would have looked foolish to many in the world in which they lived. But their actions serve as a model of faith for the rest of us to follow as they knelt before the Christ child and honored him by offering Jesus their best: gold, frankincense, and myrrh.

Maybe the story of the magi teaches us that what looks foolish in the eyes of many is often considered wise in the eyes of God. Therefore, more trips to the front yard to stand under a star and offer thanks to God might be warranted. What do you think?

A time for **building up**

"For everything there is a season, and a time for every matter under heaven:... a time to break down, and a time to build up."

Ecclesiastes 3:1,3b

My wife's sister Carol, our niece Lauren, and at the time her eighteen-month-old son Grayson came to visit Sharon and me for a weekend. Active would be an apt description of Grayson. At one point, I decided that I would entertain him by building a Lego tower just like I used to do for my three boys when they were Grayson's age. I would build a structure high enough that it was about to fall over. Then the boys would take great pleasure in knocking it down. Like many other little boys, the tower crashing to the floor was their favorite part of the activity.

I expected Grayson to react the same way. However, since he was so young, I decided he might need to be taught how to knock down the tower, so I demolished it. What I didn't expect was Grayson's reaction to the demolition. His eyes got really big. He looked at what was left of the tower. He looked at me. He looked at the scattered Legos. Then, he looked back at me and declared, "Uh-oh!"

Grayson reached for a Lego piece on the floor and placed it on the table for a foundation. He then, piece by piece, rebuilt the tower. Overcoming my initial shock from Grayson's reaction, I began helping him rebuild the tower. Not only did we rebuild it back to the original form, we built it stronger and made it far more impressive than it had been before. During the process of rebuilding, I recalled the above passage of scripture from Ecclesiastes.

For Grayson, building something up brought him far more joy than tearing something down. I rediscovered that same joy as Grayson and I worked together to build up something very special that day. I pray that you will be blessed by a season of building.

Just going to the store for a rake

"Then God said, 'Let there be light'; and there was light."

Genesis 1:3

For the most part, I believe we humans are not fans of disorder and chaos. Unpredictability and uncertainty make us anxious and fearful.

My wife Sharon asked me to take her to Home Depot to purchase a rake. This was a straightforward request that could easily be granted. All that was involved was driving her to the store, walking into the store, finding a clerk to show me the way to the rakes, and purchasing one. Then, I would drive my wife and the rake back home. I was glad to help.

However, our trip took an unexpected turn when I drove by PetSmart on the way to get the rake. A local rescue shelter had placed crates in front of the store displaying dogs and puppies for adoption. Sharon stopped to look. Instead of coming back with a rake, we returned home with a ten-week-old puppy.

To be more specific, we came home with an eight-pound Cairnoodle (half Cairn Terrier and half French

Poodle). If you believe that Elvis Presley never really died, and to this day you are on the lookout for him, I can tell you that as of that day we went to the store, you will find Elvis at our house. He bursts into high-pitched songs all hours of the day and night accompanied by gyrations that you would not believe. To say there is some angst at our house caused by eight pounds of chaos and unpredictability called Elvis is an understatement.

I believe that the need for order and predictability was in the mind of the author of Genesis when writing the story of creation:

> In the beginning when God created the heavens and the earth, the earth was a formless void [without order] and darkness [uncertainty] covered the face of the deep, while a wind from God swept over the [chaotic] face of the waters. Then God said, "Let there be light;" and there was light. And God saw that the light was good; and God separated the light from darkness [created order and predictability]. God called the light Day and the darkness he called Night. And there was evening and there was morning the first day [of creation].
>
> Gen 1:1-5

God provided the gift of order in the midst of our chaos. God gave us something we can count on to calm our fears. The darkness of night will be followed by the light of day. I interpret this divine gift to mean that a potty-trained

Cairnoodle named Elvis, who sleeps through the night, is in my future. How do you interpret this divine gift of order in the midst of the chaos you are facing today? What is the hope that God provides for you, knowing that, in Christ, our times of darkness are always followed by light?

Enough for all

"Share your bread with the hungry."

Isaiah 58:7

With birdseed spilling everywhere, I poured the contents of the bag into the two bird feeders in our backyard. Within minutes house finches, house sparrows, a mourning dove, a white-winged dove, a northern cardinal, a brown-headed cowbird, a couple of European starlings, and several squirrels converged upon the feeders and the ground below, which was covered with the overflow of seed.

However, a peaceful mealtime was interrupted by the actions of the rather large white-winged dove. This dove began lunging at the smaller mourning dove accompanied by a frantic flapping of wings and pecking at the head and body of the more diminutive bird. Clearly, the white-winged dove was communicating that there was not enough room at the supper table for the smaller dove. Yet the other guests at the banquet seemed perfectly content to share.

My thought upon watching this drama unfold around the bird feeder was that the white-winged dove's actions seemed foolish in the midst of plenty of food for all. Is this a window through which we might see our own human flaws? Do we contradict God's call to love our neighbor each time we let our fear of scarcity determine our thoughts and actions, even when there are plenty of basic necessities of life to go around?

> "Is it not [the right thing] to share your bread
> with the hungry,
> and to bring the homeless poor into your house;
> when you see the naked, to cover them,
> and not to hide yourself from your own kin?
> Then your light shall break forth like the dawn;
> the glory of the Lord shall be your rear guard."
>
> Isa 58:7-8

A pair of wet socks

"'What do you think? Which one of these three was a neighbor to the man who encountered thieves?' Then the legal expert said, 'The one who demonstrated mercy toward him.' Jesus told him, 'Go and do likewise.'"

Luke 10:36-37 CEB

Our then ten-year-old son, Stephen, was upset that his soccer uniform was still in the washer minutes before we had to leave for his game. A brief interlude in the dryer was a tremendous help with the shirt and pants. However, his socks were soaking wet when we jumped into the car.

I thought it was a stroke of genius when I decided to roll up the passenger side window to serve as a make-shift clasp allowing the socks to flap in the breeze, drying on the way to the soccer field. Stephen was skeptical, to say the least, as to the effectiveness of this new drying technique. He looked at the socks fluttering in the wind and then turned to look at me. He spoke, matter-of-factly, "Sometimes you are just not very responsible, are you?"

When Jesus told the parable about two prominent men of faith who bypassed a wounded traveler without offering a helping hand, he was saying to his listeners,

"Sometimes you are just not very responsible, are you?" (see Luke 10:25-37).

Jesus asked his disciples to watch and pray as he entered the Garden of Gethsemane. He returned to find the disciples sleeping. When he asked them, "Why are you sleeping? Get up and pray" (Luke 22:46), wasn't Jesus really saying to his followers, "Sometimes you are just not very responsible, are you?"

When Jesus, hanging on a Roman cross, cried out, "Father, forgive them, for they do not know what they are doing" (Luke 23:34), he was simply saying to God, "Sometimes your people are just not very responsible, are they?"

Just as Jesus reminded his followers of old when they were not being very responsible, I believe that he still reaches through the thin veil between heaven and earth to remind us today when we are not being very responsible. Over the years, I have come to understand that true spiritual transformation and growth does not take place until we can see clearly that which needs to change in us. Only by the grace of God through faith can we have eyes to see our sin and shortcomings. Then, by grace we are led down a path toward forgiveness, healthier choices, and new life in Christ.

Let us pray to our Lord this week for eyes to see our wet socks flailing in the breeze, so that we might make the choice to live more responsibly as his followers.

A memorable baptism

"[Jesus] replied, 'Truly I tell you, today you will be with me in Paradise.'"

Luke 23:43

A friend's nine-year-old grandson at the time, Brett, has a very special dog named Oscar, a great name for a dachshund. Brett's love for Oscar caused him to consider that, when he and his family go to heaven someday, he wanted to be sure that Oscar would join them. So Brett decided this meant Oscar needed to be baptized. He invited his whole family into the bathroom where he had filled the bathtub with water. He stepped into the tub, wearing his bathing suit and carrying Oscar. At the last second, he decided that the United Methodist practice of sprinkling would work better for Oscar than the Baptist practice of immersion. Brett asked, "Oscar, do you accept Jesus Christ as your Savior?" Brett barked twice to indicate that Oscar said, "I do." Then, while sprinkling water on Oscar's head, Brett declared, "Oscar, I baptize you in the name of the Father, Son, and Holy Spirit. Amen." Of course, Brett had to repeat this ritual three more times so that the parents and grandparents could capture the moment on camera and video.

I am not suggesting that we all need to head to the nearest bathtub with our pets. However, I do believe that the love that led Brett to take care of a family member's spiritual need is something very special. Jesus tended to the spiritual needs of God's family, whether that meant forgiving sins (see Mark 2:5) or inviting another to join him "in Paradise" (Luke 23:43). He, like Brett, wanted to be sure that no one was left behind when it came to matters of our eternal relationship with God and family. Thank you, Brett, for reminding us of that which is of ultimate significance.

Just **feeding** the fish

"Do not be afraid; from now on you will be catching people."

Luke 5:10

When I load up the car with my fishing pole (a hook and bobber attached to the line) and a handful of earthworms, unnamed persons have suggested that I am headed out to feed the fish and not catch them. I choose to ignore such half-truths (perhaps a little more truth than not) because of the overwhelming joy I experience as I anticipate sitting on the bank of a pond or stream, enjoying the quiet beauty of God's creation.

We read in the New Testament about a professional fisherman, Simon Peter, who knows something about how to catch fish. The story begins with him fishing all night but not catching anything. Jesus tells him to try one more time. On Jesus' command, Simon catches so many fish that he needs several of his fishing buddies to help haul the loaded nets up onto their boats. Simon's obedience leads to an amazing experience of abundance. And everyone participated!

This story captures three aspects of life at St. Andrew. First, Simon's obedience was an expression of worship. Second, it happened in community. When we obey Jesus as Simon did, we will experience abundance along with our family and friends.

Third, there is a twist to the story. It seems that fishing involves feeding as well as catching. After the abundant haul of fish, Jesus said to Simon Peter and his friends, "From now on you will be catching people" (Luke 5:10).

Of course, Jesus was not suggesting that the disciples use a net, hooks, or worms to catch people. Instead, Jesus would say to feed people the good news of God's redeeming love. Feasting on God's love will cause persons to want to feed others by casting wide the net of God's unconditional love so that, someday, all might know the quiet beauty of living in God's loving presence. Jesus' call to "fish for people" is actually a call to serve God and others by daily feeding others with the love of Christ.

Doing life alone

"[Jesus] replied, 'What is impossible for mortals is possible for God.'"

Luke 18:27

My guess is that your annual New Year's covenants/resolutions are challenged by a variety of both anticipated and unexpected life circumstances. What can you and I do to get back on track (or to stay on track) when it comes to following through on personal goals for each New Year?

My best and only suggestion is don't go it alone. Remember, we were created by God to do life together. That means trusting in God's grace to stay the course regarding our resolutions while drawing upon the love and support of family and friends.

I came to a deeper understanding of this one Sunday near the New Year. An envelope was given to me by a member of our church family. It contained New Year's covenants/resolutions of each member of that family. In a first for me, they requested that I pray over each one.

As I read and prayed, I realized the wisdom of this family's approach. They wrote their resolutions together (each could choose to keep theirs confidential or share them with the family). This communal act served as a reminder that they are not alone in visioning something better for themselves or others in the New Year. The fact that each family member knew their covenant/resolution was being offered up to God in prayer by another provided further assurance that both divine and additional human help was available to them to accomplish their vision for that year.

So, if you have not done so already, give yourself the best opportunity to fulfill your New Year's covenant/resolutions by adding an extra-large helping of prayer, and by inviting a group of supportive friends and family members to help you stay the course.

We are blessed to have a God and a faith community that wants the best for us and wants us to be the best for others. Let's count on these blessings to help us make each New Year the best year ever!

The dumpster miracle

"All of you are one in Christ Jesus."

Galatians 3:28

It's a long story, but my notes for a major paper in seminary ended up in my dorm's dumpster. I jumped in to rescue them. While searching through the garbage, my friend Tom saw me. He came over to the dumpster and asked, "Hasley, what in the world are you doing in this dumpster?" I explained and the next thing I knew Tom had put his books down on the sidewalk and jumped into the dumpster with me. We looked and looked until we found my notes at the bottom of that dumpster.

Now you might think that the miracle on that day was finding my notes, which were crucial for completing a paper for a major grade in a theology class. That was not the real miracle that took place, however. The miracle was that Tom and I solidified a friendship that we did not have growing up together in Magnolia, Arkansas.

Tom and I grew up on different sides of the tracks. Therefore, we never crossed paths. He went to the high school with the other black students in town. I went to the high school with the other white kids. It was not until we attended Perkins School of Theology in Dallas and jumped into a dumpster together that we became good friends. Sometimes you have to sort through a lot of garbage—like racism, bigotry, and prejudice—before you come to the place where you love your neighbor as our Lord created us to do.

May the Lord help you sort through the trash in your life and get to a place where you can honor and glorify the Lord by loving your neighbor.

A nail salon Easter story

"For I am convinced that neither death, nor life, nor angels, nor rulers, nor things present, nor things to come, nor powers, nor height, nor depth, nor anything else in all creation, will be able to separate us from the love of God in Christ Jesus our Lord."

Romans 8:38-39

A young mom brought her eight-year-old daughter and four-year-old son with her to the nail salon just before Easter weekend. The mom and the daughter were scheduled for manicures and pedicures. The four-year-old boy was expected to wait.

Now, for a four-year-old to wait a few minutes—without a playmate and no room to do what little boys do like run, jump, and burn off energy—is one thing. However, to have to sit for an entire hour in a crowded nail salon without a playmate and with no room to roam is another matter altogether. He immediately became fidgety. The longer he had to wait, the more painful and agonizing the experience became.

Toward the end of the hour, with a dark cloud of despair hanging over him, the boy walked over to the only other male in the salon, a young man who was staffing the front desk. The boy stood next to the receptionist hoping for some interaction that would relieve his boredom. Then the boy watched a client walk up to the front. She opened her purse and handed the young man at the desk some money. The client turned and walked out of the salon.

The boy's eyes became as big as saucers. With a look of unadulterated fear in his eyes, he shouted for all in the nail salon to hear: "Wait. You mean you have to pay to get out of here?" The receptionist, joking around with the boy, responded, "Of course you have to pay to get out of here. Do you have any money?"

With a look of utter despair on his face, the four-year-old shook his head no. At that moment, he was overwhelmed with the horrific thought that he might have to spend the rest of his life in that nail salon.

Like this young boy, there are times when we feel trapped by circumstances beyond our control. Feelings of helplessness, isolation, and despair can overwhelm us to the point that we cannot see a way out.

The message of Easter is that the darkness of despair has been overcome by the hope of the Risen Christ. As the Apostle Paul reminds us, not even the darkness of death can separate us from the love of God as revealed through Jesus Christ our Lord.

Jesus has already paid the price on the cross for us to get out of dark places of despair and to move toward the light of hope. All we must do is take his hand and follow his lead.

Donuts and monster trucks

"Let the little children come to me."

Luke 18:16

At the 8:00 a.m. contemporary worship service one Easter morning, young parents were led into worship by their two-year-old son, Travis. Travis walked up and informed me that the Easter bunny had come to his house.

On cue, I asked, "What did the Easter bunny bring you?"

With a grin that reached from ear to ear, Travis replied, "Donuts."

Expecting the answer to be "eggs," I was caught off guard. So I tried again: "What else did the Easter bunny bring?"

Again, Travis smiled and, with a twinkle in his eye, said, "Monster trucks!"

My immediate thought was that the Easter bunny has expanded his business significantly. Back in the day, the Easter bunny came and hid eggs for children to find. Now, the Easter bunny is in the donut and monster truck business as well.

I love interacting with young children. Their unadulterated joy over the simplest things, like donuts, is refreshing. Their creative minds have no room for fear of change; instead, they embrace innovation and the unexpected. What did Jesus say?

> "Truly I tell you, whoever does not receive
> the kingdom of God as a little child
> will never enter it."
>
> Luke 18:17

Pray with me today: "Lord, may today be a 'donut and monster truck kind of day' full of divine surprises, such as encountering and sharing the love of the Risen Christ. Amen."

An angel of hope

“But the angel said to the women, ‘Do not be afraid.’”

Matthew 28:5

I have a friend who is one of the most positive persons I have ever had the privilege to meet. She was told recently that she was of the age and stage in life that independent living was no longer possible. My friend gave me a phone call to tell me the news. She unconvincingly said that everything was going to be all right.

So I took a road trip to visit my friend and, again, she informed me that everything was going to be all right. However, she said it this time with conviction and a twinkle in her eye. Then she told me what had lifted here spirit between our initial phone conversation and my visit.

One of the caregivers at the long-term care facility where she is now staying looked directly at her and said, “You have lost hope, haven’t you?” Before my friend could answer, the caregiver asked if it would be all right if she read a passage or two from the Bible which was on the bedside stand. After reading the Bible, the caregiver held my friend in her arms, prayed for her, and said, “Don’t lose hope. You never know what wonderful things the Lord has in store for you, even at this time and in this place!”

Clearly, this caregiver was an angel of hope for my

friend, just as my friend has been an angel of hope for me. Maybe that is the best description of our purpose in life as people of faith. We are to be angels (which means messengers) of hope for others. For whom might you be a messenger of hope today?

Placing limits on compassion

"The Lord is good to all, / and his compassion is over all that he has made."

Psalm 145:9

I was called to the hospital by a friend whose wife had gone into labor with their first child. Stopping by the labor and delivery room, I let Jim and Margie, the expectant couple, know that I would be in the waiting room. However, before I could exit the doorway, Jim called out in his booming voice, "Come on in!"

I vehemently protested, but Jim would not listen. He pulled me into the room and sat me in the chair next to the bed. Then, he revealed that there was paperwork he needed to complete at the admissions desk. Before I could say anything, Jim was out the door, and there I sat with Margie whose contractions were growing stronger by the minute.

I was already the father of three, so I had been through Lamaze classes. When the labor became very strong with short intervals between contractions, I began coaching Margie on her breathing while stroking her arm. The delivery went well. However, I never let Jim forget that I helped bring his firstborn into the world. Furthermore, I told him delivery of a child was not in my job description as either his pastor or friend! That was my way of letting him know that I had boundaries when it came to shepherding my flock.

The more I think about that pastoral moment over the years, the more I am convinced that you cannot put limits around compassion. As Jesus exemplified in his life, teachings, and death on a cross, compassion requires a willingness to pay the price (to sacrifice) to meet the need of God's children. To be compassionate means to be willing to experience pain and discomfort to act on the love of God and love of neighbor. God so loved the world that he was willing to experience the pain and sacrifice of giving up his only begotten Son, so that whoever believed in him would not perish, but would have life eternal (based on John 3:16).

Jesus taught us that there are no boundaries when it comes to showing compassion toward others. In fact, just the opposite is true. God's love for his people is without boundaries. As God's hands and feet, we are called to be compassionate servants of Jesus Christ.

Making life worth living

"You are the light of the world."

Matthew 5:14

My Aunt Emogene was the last of my father's eleven brothers and sisters to pass into the Lord's heavenly kingdom. All of them grew up on a small farm in Arkansas. At the funeral in Gurdon, Arkansas, I shared a story about how Uncle Buddy and Aunt Emogene had introduced themselves at a church function. Uncle Buddy stood up and introduced himself as the bread winner of the family. Then Aunt Emogene stood up. With a wide grin on her face and her index finger pointing at her husband, Aunt Emogene declared: "He makes the living and I make life worth living."

She sat down to robust applause and tons of laughter. Aunt Emogene's introduction of herself that day was an accurate description of what she brought to a relationship.

As a lifelong active member of First United Methodist Church in Gurdon, Aunt Emogene was a person of deep faith and impeccable moral standards. Everyone who knew her described her as an incredibly kind, compassionate, and caring individual who would do anything to help a family member, friend, or neighbor in need. She would light up any room that she entered with her phenomenal smile and joyful laughter.

I accepted a calling to full-time ministry in large part due to the example that Aunt Emogene provided to me as a follower of Jesus Christ. Her impact on my family and me can be seen in the fact that my eighteen-month-old granddaughter has been named Emogene after my aunt. In my eyes as her Papaw, my granddaughter lights up any room she enters, just as Aunt Emogene did.

Take a moment to reflect on the people in your life who have made or who are making life worth living. Offer up a prayer of thanks to the Lord for their impact on your life. Then reflect for a moment what you might do or say to help make life worth living for someone else.

Now, go and light up a room or two in the name of Christ.

Chasing the star

"After Jesus was born in Bethlehem of Judea, wise men from the East came to Jerusalem, asking, 'Where is the child who has been born king of the Jews? For we observed his star at its rising, and have come to pay him homage.'"

Matthew 2:1-2

Project Hope is a significant component of the outreach of The Storehouse of Collin County, providing coaching and mentoring to single mothers who are committed to breaking free from the cycle of poverty, abandonment, and abuse. We had a great Christmas party one evening, provided by volunteers, and followed by testimonies from friends (clients) of Project Hope.

The time came for the Christmas story, reenacted by the children of the friends of Project Hope. The narrator read from the Gospel of Luke about Mary giving birth to baby Jesus in Bethlehem. Two of the children entered the room dressed as Joseph and Mary. Mary wrapped baby Jesus up in swaddling clothes and placed him in a manger. A donkey with floppy ears observed the proceedings.

Next, the narrator declared that an angel appeared to the shepherds announcing that, in the City of David, a Savior had been born, who is Christ the Lord. Children carrying shepherds' crooks arrived at the manger followed by several very timid children in sheep's clothing.

From the Gospel of Matthew, we heard about the magi following the star to the place where Jesus was born. However, the magi at the Project Hope Christmas party found that following the star was easier said than done. The child who was dressed as the star moved as fast as he possibly could around the room, while the magi did everything in their power to keep up with that speeding star. The star eventually stopped next to the manger. The magi arrived a little later with hands on their knees, attempting to catch their breath.

This reenactment of the magi following the star will certainly be forever remembered by all who witnessed it. But the reenactment also highlighted an important truth about our faith. To follow a path illuminated by the light of God's unconditional love is not an easy assignment. To be able to love unconditionally like God loves takes the grace of God and a lot of hard work and sacrifice on our part. But the Christmas story tells us that the journey of faith is well worth the effort.

At Christmas and all year long, I pray that you will trust in God's grace and do whatever you must to follow the light of God's love to the manger in Bethlehem. If you stay the course and encounter the full impact of Christ's love and grace, I believe that your heart will be changed. The joy, love, and hope that will fill your heart is the true gift of Christmas.

Doing life the Jesus way

"Jesus said to him, 'What do you want me to do for you?'"

Mark 10:51

Sometime ago, I heard Peter share his faith journey, which led him to become a youth worker for Christ in his home country of Bangladesh. For Peter, the life and work of Jesus became the model for his ministry. He believes that Jesus' lifework was a ministry of listening to the needs of others, looking for the needs of others, and responding to meet those needs.

Jesus' disciples heard the cries for help of a blind man named Bartimaeus. Yet they attempted to quiet his pleas. However, when Jesus heard the blind man's cries, he listened, observed, and responded to his needs.

Most of the crowd that gathered to get a glimpse of Jesus did not notice Zacchaeus climb up the sycamore tree. However, Jesus not only saw Zacchaeus, he listened to him, and invited him to repent of his self-serving ways and to follow the pathway of divine, loving service.

When it comes to doing what God requires of us as his followers, Peter, the youth worker from Bangladesh, reminded me that Jesus teaches us in the name of the Lord God to:

-listen to the needs of our neighbors;
-look for the need;
-respond to the need.

Embracing Christ's pattern of serving frees us all to be the passionate servants of Jesus Christ that we are created to be. Just like Peter inspired and encouraged me, let us work side by side to encourage each other to be all that God calls us to be by listening, looking, and responding.

A blessing from Callie

"Let the words of my mouth and the meditation of my heart / be acceptable to you, / O Lord, my rock and my redeemer."

Psalm 19:14

From the moment of her baptism at First United Methodist Church of Magnolia, Arkansas, I have watched my niece, Callie Bailey, grow in her relationship with Christ. Callie wrote the following poem at the age of seventeen. This is just the latest sign that she is growing up very quickly. Enjoy!

Freedom in Christ

We're all slaves to something, vice or sin
We're all fighting a battle that we alone can't win

When hate bars our hearts
And shame chains our souls

The weight of the world is too heavy
And we've lost all control

We yearn for freedom in knowledge, appearance,
or wealth
But we will never be able to break these chains
by ourselves

For freedom cannot be found in anything of this earth
The story of true freedom begins with the virgin birth

And is solidified with the ultimate sacrifice of Christ
He gave his life to save us from eternal strife

Our Savior is the truth, the light, the way
And he set our souls free when he died that solemn day

The world once lived in darkness
But now bursts forth in living color

An unencumbered life through Christ
Compares to no other

For when I chose to follow him
He broke the bonds of fear and sin

Now love fills my heart
And joy surrounds my soul

The weight of the world is lifted
And God has control

I finally know what it means to be free
Freedom is living in Christ

And letting Christ live in me

Callie Bailey

God is with us

"For I am convinced that neither death, nor life... will be able to separate us from the love of God in Christ Jesus our Lord."

Romans 8:38-39

After seventeen nights trapped in a dark cave, all the members of a Thai youth soccer team and their coach were freed by a Thai-led international rescue team in July 2018. People from around the world were united in prayer for the health and well-being of the Wild Boar Soccer Team and their rescuers.

As I sought to find appropriate words for my prayers, I recalled the events around the rescue of eighteen-month-old Baby Jessica in 1987. She fell into a well in her aunt's backyard in Midland, Texas, and rescuers worked for fifty-eight hours to successfully rescue her from the eight-inch well casing.

One Sunday during the rescue operation, I asked a large group of children who were gathered for worship at St. Andrew, "Where is God while Baby Jessica is trapped in that hole?" One child raised his hand and, without hesitation, said, "God is down there in that hole with Baby Jessica." The St. Andrew family was blessed that Sunday by a child's reassuring faith.

Therefore, my prayer for the soccer team, their coach, and the rescue workers over the two weeks they were trapped was, "Lord, please help them to know that you are in that dark, damp cave with them. May the families, also, know the strength of your presence, especially the family members of the courageous diver who lost his life in the rescue attempt."

I thank the Lord for the words of the child who reminded us years ago of the eternal truth that God is with us always, especially in the darkest times of our lives when we feel trapped and alone.

To whom do you belong?

"For last night there stood by me an angel of the God to whom I belong and whom I worship."

Acts 27:23

Students in the St. Andrew Confirmation Class hand out Bibles to our third graders each year. Receiving their own Bibles with their names in them is a sacred rite of passage for our children on their spiritual journeys to becoming lifelong followers of Christ.

A mother of a third grader who had received her Bible at St. Andrew years before approached me with a story about her daughter. She let me know how meaningful it was to her daughter to be given a Bible by her faith family with her name inside. The fact that her name was in her Bible was a reminder that she belonged to God.

Her daughter went off to college, where her friendship circle was tempting her to turn to drugs for fun and enjoyment. While contemplating this path of drug use, she turned an eye toward her bookshelf where sat her third-grade Bible. Her Bible reminded her that her life belonged to God, and she decided to honor God by choosing not to follow the path of drug use.

Her mom's eyes filled with tears as she thanked me for the St. Andrew faith family whose gift of the third-grade

Bible served to help guide her daughter away from a dark path. Instead, she proudly shared with me how her daughter was now in one of the outstanding medical schools in the country, studying to become a physical therapist.

I asked her if I could tell her daughter's story. She said, of course I could share it, with the hope that her story would have a positive impact upon other students who might be tempted to go down the path of drug use. "Maybe," she said, "my daughter's story will remind someone else to whom their life belongs."

Both full and empty

"Worship the Lord your God, / and serve only him."

Matthew 4:10

I have just returned from a phenomenal trip led by Scott and Patti Engle to the Holy Land which began in Rome, Italy. While in Rome, I learned a great deal about the nature of the Roman occupiers during Jesus' day. The Roman Empire was, on the one hand, advanced beyond any society that had come before it. From long-lasting roads, aqueducts, residences, government facilities, and temples to military and political might and wealth, the Roman Empire stood apart from all others. Historians wrote that theirs was a society full of abundance, which provided a model for all to emulate.

On the other hand, the Roman Empire of Jesus' day was also empty. The worship of idols and, over time, the worship of Caesar led to a society driven by power, wealth, and prestige. The lack of value placed on human life, exemplified by enslavement of conquered people; the scorched earth policy in response to criminals, rebellions, and perceived threats (e.g. Jesus' crucifixion); and eventually the martyrdom of Christians in the Coliseum, revealed a society short on virtues and lacking a moral compass.

Even today, in the midst of our celebration of the fullness and the blessings of our lives, we recognize that virtues and morality are often sacrificed in the pursuit of the acquisition of power, wealth, and prestige.

Jesus' response to this untenable dichotomy is to challenge us to seek a congruent life. Jesus, who loves us unconditionally, declares, "Worship the Lord your God, / and serve only him" (Matt 4:10).

Later in the Gospel of Matthew, Jesus teaches, "You shall love the Lord your God with all your heart, and with all your soul, and with all your mind.... You shall love your neighbor as yourself" (Matt 22:37,39).

Let us open our ears to hear. In order to live a full and abundant life we must trust in God's amazing grace, turn away from worshiping all that brings emptiness, and choose instead to worship and serve only the Lord our God by loving God and our neighbor as ourselves.

An abundance of hope

"'Look, the virgin will conceive and bear a son, / and they shall name him Emmanuel,' which means, 'God is with us.'"

Matthew 1:23

Over ten years ago, St. Andrew was introduced to the Cabécar community, an indigenous people living on a reservation in the Talamanca mountains in southeastern Costa Rica. I was initially struck by a general lack of eye contact and lack of facial expression, especially smiles. Over time, I began to better understand their strong lack of responsiveness to people outside their community. There was a huge language barrier; many Cabécars speak and understand only their native language. Additionally, the Cabécars are isolated geographically in the Talamanca mountains.

I also began to witness the daily discrimination the Cabécars faced. Many of the basic government services we take for granted in this country were not made readily available to the Cabécars. There was an inadequate (in some cases, nonexistent) road/bridge system to access the Cabécar villages. Therefore, reaching the villages meant crossing rivers and streams by foot or with four-wheel drive vehicles. Drownings were not uncommon for those crossing on foot due to unpredictable currents and high water levels.

There was no electricity on the reservation, with many families cooking on wood-burning stoves inside unvented homes. A natural consequence has been pulmonary health issues related to smoke inhalation.

Availability of adequate health care was a longstanding issue among the Cabécars, with their only medical clinic (government operated) located at the base of the mountain. The clinic was open for only limited hours and had a sparse supply of medications. It was not uncommon for Cabécar patients to walk two days to reach the clinic for treatment, only to discover that the clinic was either closed or out of the medication they needed. Access to dependable, quality medical care was the number one need expressed by the chief of Jabuy, the Cabécar village.

When we told the chief that we would work alongside them to make quality year-round health care available to the Cabécar people, he responded with one question:"How will you be different than those who have gone before you? Most have come, offered, and failed to follow through."

We replied, "By the grace of God, we will help you to build, staff, and operate a clinic." Now, a clinic we call Clínica Emanuel (God with Us) is fully operational in Jabuy. Lives are being improved and saved each week by an outstanding Costa Rican medical staff, all for the glory of God and out of love for all of God's children.

During a recent visit to Jabuy by a St. Andrew mission team, I was asked by Lilliana, the Clínica Emanuel manager, if I had noticed the smiles on the Cabécars' faces and the twinkle in their eyes. I nodded and replied that the transformation must have resulted from bridges being built, roads improved, electricity provided, and the establishment of the clinic. Lilliana explained the reason for the smiles with words that I will never forget: "The Lord is here."

Battling monsters

"'The Lord,' David added, 'who rescued me from the power of both lions and bears, will rescue me from the power of this Philistine.'

'Go!' Saul replied to David. 'And may the Lord be with you!'"

1 Samuel 17:37 (CEB)

My grandnephews and grandnieces (ages two–six) were becoming increasingly restless while waiting for their food at the upscale restaurant. I suggested, "Let's go on an adventure."

They immediately grabbed my arm and told me that we were hunting for Lava Monsters. All four proceeded to describe the behemoths to me. They taught me that Lava Monsters have the capacity to change colors, much like a chameleon. The one we spotted was orange. Then, I was informed, it became yellow. Finally, it changed to red. Additionally, I learned that a Lava Monster is extremely tall. Lily shared with me that a Lava Monster can be as tall as I am. Lily, Abby, Corbin, and Jack corrected themselves, letting me know that they are as tall as heaven. Finally, they all agreed that Lava Monsters are as tall as the universe.

However, based on the look on their faces and tone of their voices, what was absolutely true is that a Lava Monster is scary and dangerous. According to Corbin, the only way to stop this monster was a karate kick to the stomach. He was confident that he could deliver the fatal blow if the Lava Monster ever threatened us. Lily, Abby, and Jack nodded in agreement.

I wonder what it would be like to have their courage and confidence when facing monsters such as fear, hate, hopelessness, and loss that daily threaten spiritual, emotional, and physical health and well-being.

There is a story about an Old Testament personality named David who, as a very young warrior, courageously faced a monster called Goliath. David declared to King Saul that God was the source of his confidence and strength to face and defeat the giant.

My fervent prayer is that, by God's grace through faith, you will be delivered from the fear of all monsters (including Lava Monsters) that threaten to diminish your life. May God, through Christ Jesus, give you the courage to face and overcome all monsters according to God's will.

The crack of the bat

"King of kings and Lord of Lords."

Revelation 19:16

A year and a half ago, I flew with my three sons, Stephen, John, and Will to Phoenix, Arizona, to watch the Texas Rangers participate in spring training. As we exited the rental car to walk to the field where the Rangers were playing an afternoon game, the sound I heard was a baseball bat connecting with the ball as the players took batting practice prior to a game. With the first crack of the bat, memories flooded my mind. I recalled watching a game with my dad in Yankee Stadium where both Mickey Mantle and Roger Maris got hits against the Kansas City Athletics. I remembered the sound of the hits that my sons and I witnessed during their childhood as the Rangers battled for a championship ring. Together we watched Mike Hargrove, Al Oliver, Mickey Rivers, Juan Gonzalez, Alex Rodriquez, Pudge Rodriguez, Michael Young, and Adrian Beltré attempt to knock the cover off the ball.

That sweet sound of a bat connecting with a baseball opened my memory banks to the joy on the faces of my boys and my daughter who, over many years, stood up to cheer for their home team. I remember the cherry and grape snow cones transforming their faces into red and purple works of art. Ketchup and mustard stains on their Texas Ranger T-shirts resulted from consuming multiple hotdogs during a game. I can picture the child-sized baseball gloves that they wore in hope of catching a ball off the bat of one of their favorite players.

The crack of the bat is, for me, not only a sign that spring has arrived; that sound ignites memories of cherished relationships enjoyed over years of watching baseball together. The primary reason I love the sounds of baseball is the fond memories of spending time together with those I love.

Even more significant to me than the crack of the bat is a powerful sound of faith that marks for me that spring has arrived. This musical piece evokes memories of spending time with those I love in worship of the Risen Lord. Of course, I am referring to singing the "Hallelujah" Chorus from Handel's Messiah on Easter Sunday. Handel was a devout Christian and his Messiah reflects the depth of his faith. The closing lines from the "Hallelujah" Chorus read:

"And He shall reign forever and ever,
King of kings and Lord of Lords,
And He shall reign forever and ever
King of kings and Lord of Lords,
Hallelujah! Hallelujah! Hallelujah!
Hallelujah! Hallelujah!"

The primary reason I like this phenomenal music is my love for Jesus Christ and my love for my family, including my extended family of faith. When I sing the "Hallelujah" Chorus, I can envision the joy on the faces of my children, along with our St. Andrew children, as they stand in their Easter clothes to sing and celebrate. On Easter, we celebrate, not a baseball victory that lasts only to the next game; but we celebrate our victory in Christ, which lasts for all eternity.

An Ash Wednesday surprise

"I… repent in dust and ashes."

Job 42:6

As an associate pastor at Highland Park United Methodist Church, I felt honored to be assigned to lead the upcoming Ash Wednesday worship service, marking the beginning of the Lenten season. What I failed to comprehend was that leading meant not only preaching but also ordering the ashes to be imposed during the service. Not until dawn on Ash Wednesday did I realize that I did not have ashes for the service that night. Furthermore, I quickly found out it was too late to order them from the liturgical supply store.

Therefore, I set Plan B into motion. I asked a member of the church facilities staff to do whatever he could to locate ashes to use to impose a cross on the forehead of the worshipers that evening at 7:00 p.m. Meanwhile, I found a secluded spot in the church to review and practice my sermon. I returned to my office around mid-afternoon to discover that a smoldering paper sack had been placed on my desk containing white-hot ashes. I quickly placed the smoking sack into a metal trash can by my desk, just in case the paper bag caught fire. Fortunately, by the time the Ash Wednesday service rolled around, the ashes had cooled down enough that I could use them. I was ecstatic that plan B had worked.

My first clue that my plan had not worked as well as I originally thought came by phone the next morning. A worshiper from the night before informed me that, following the service, a rash in the shape of a cross had appeared on his forehead exactly where the ashes had been imposed. Subsequent calls and office visits echoed that report.

Now, I chose not to tell the staff member who had so willingly delivered the ashes to my office what had transpired. I thought it better not to know what material he had burned to produce the "sacred" ashes. However, I did choose to see the positives coming out of that Ash Wednesday worship service. First, the cross-shaped rash that broke out that night on the foreheads of the worshipers provided a tremendous opportunity to be a witness the following day to our crucified and Risen Lord. Second, this Ash Wednesday service opened my eyes to a "fresh new approach" to the practice of spiritual disciplines during Lent in preparation for the celebration of our Risen Lord. Finally, like my mom used to say to me, "Confession is good for the soul." I have finally accomplished that with this writing!

The gift of empathy

"Rejoice with those who rejoice, weep with those who weep."

Romans 12:15

Simply defined, empathy is the projection of one's persona into another's experiences to understand better another person's emotions, thoughts, or feelings. I am aware that there is an ongoing debate as to whether such a projection is possible. Can a person realistically put themselves into the shoes of another person? I believe that the barriers to true empathy are formidable. But do the barriers to empathy mean we don't try to empathize with the plight of another person? For me, the answer to this question is a resounding no. We must make the effort to be empathic if we are ever to come close to emulating the love and compassion of Jesus Christ. There is a story from my past that has brought me to this conclusion.

Don McMahen was my high school principal in Magnolia, Arkansas. He was a man of deep faith who was greatly loved and highly respected for his compassion and integrity. The summer that our school system integrated, Mr. McMahen called together the members of the Magnolia High School Student Council. He loaded us on a bus and took us to Columbia High School from which the black students would be bussed to the all-white Magnolia High School.

When we arrived, the Columbia High Student Council welcomed us and proceeded to give us a tour of their school. They showed us their classrooms and told us stories about the teachers who had impacted their lives in transformational ways. They took us to the gymnasium where they recounted the many state basketball championships they had won. Then we were led to the cafeteria and the auditorium. Stories of friendships made and memories created were shared with us there. They walked us back to the bus, and we all said our goodbyes.

Once we were back on the bus, Mr. McMahen had the driver close the door, and he stood up to speak. In his own humble, homespun way, he challenged us that day to put ourselves in the shoes of the Columbia High School students. "What if you were the one who had been told you would no longer be attending the high school you had long anticipated to attend?" he asked. "Instead, what if you were told that you would be transported across town to an unfamiliar high school, while the school you loved and cared about would be bulldozed to the ground? How would you feel if you knew you had to leave behind the teachers who had compassionately shaped and molded your life?" he inquired. "Instead, you were required to be taught by teachers who were strangers to you, and you were strangers to them. How would you respond to leaving behind your mascot, your motto, your school song, your yearbook, your unique identity to become a part of an identity that you had neither chosen nor desired?"

That day was the first time I opened my eyes to the stark reality of racial injustice. It was an extremely troubling and uncomfortable experience, but Mr. McMahen made it crystal clear by his empathic act that our discomfort was nothing compared to the pain, disappointment, and anger that the Columbia High School students were experiencing.

True empathy is almost impossible yet also essential if wrongs are to be made right. Jesus said that he had come to bring sight to the blind and to set at liberty those who are oppressed (see Luke 4:18).

Jesus saves

"Everyone who calls on the name of the Lord shall be saved."

Romans 10:13

For those of us who have grown up in the church, "Jesus saves" is a well-known affirmation of faith. Yet, when asked to explain what this means, we often stumble in our attempt to answer. A theological explanation of "Jesus saves" might read something like this:

> From the moment in the Garden of Eden when Adam and Eve chose to place their self-serving desires over God's will and desire for humankind, there has been a separation between God and us called sin. Instead of turning away from us, God chose, out of love, to pursue creation and restore a right relationship between God and us. As written in the Gospel of John, "For God so loved the world that he gave his only Son, so that everyone who believes in him may not perish but may have eternal life" (John 3:16). By faith through grace, Jesus saves us from eternal separation from God. Therefore, as followers of Christ, we have an eternal relationship with God who loves us and calls us to love and serve God with all of our heart,

soul, mind, and strength, and to love our neighbor as ourselves.

Then there is the explanation of "Jesus saves" based on life experience. A member of our congregation told me about a conversation she recently had with a clerk at a nearby store. The clerk asked, "Don't I know you?"

The church member replied, "I believe I have seen you as well." They concluded that they had seen each other at St. Andrew.

The clerk then proceeded to tell the customer that St. Andrew had "saved her life." When she was at her lowest point, she turned to St. Andrew for food and clothing, which she received from the Seven Loaves Food Pantry and Joseph's Coat. Then she said, "I have this job because of St. Andrew."

Of course, St. Andrew hadn't saved this woman's life; Jesus saved her life as God used our church as an instrument of the saving and redeeming love of Jesus Christ. Yes, "Jesus saves" when we choose to boldly proclaim the Easter story that Christ has risen; therefore, the saving love and grace of our Lord is alive and well through the work of the Lord's church.

Everything will be all right

"And my God will fully satisfy every need of yours according to his riches in glory in Christ Jesus."

Philippians 4:19

When I skinned my knee, she said it. When I had a disagreement with a classmate, she said it. When I was discouraged, she said it. "Everything will be all right," my mom would say as she gave me a hug. On numerous occasions, my grandmother echoed the very same words in the variation that serves as the book's title: *Everything Is Gonna Be All Right.* When I was very young, these few words served as a source of great comfort and encouragement. But as I got older, I dismissed these words as just something parents say, like, "I'll kiss it and make it better." I grew to believe that the phrase "everything will be all right" was just words with no grounding in reality. There were things happening in the world in general, and in my world in particular, that were telling me everything was not all right. As a matter of fact, all of society's brokenness was not going to be all right anytime soon, if ever.

However, a few months ago I came across Grandmother Stephens' Bible. Along with a brief family genealogy, she had scribbled some notes on the first few blank pages. Upon the death of Vernon Stephens, her husband of fifty years and my grandfather, she had written, "The Lord in his Infinite Mercy has granted us fifty years together for which I give him eternal thanks. Someday we shall be together again in our eternal home—along with our children." In her written words, I again heard, "everything will be all right." During the last few weeks of her battle with terminal cancer, my mom motioned for me to sit beside her. She then said, "Robert, I have fulfilled my God-given purpose on earth, which was to raise you and your sisters. I am at peace." She had just told me not to worry because "everything will be all right."

I now realize that, for my mom and grandmother, the phrase "everything will be all right" was not just a parental platitude but an affirmation of faith. Their worldview was shaped by their belief that the Lord was always watching over them and their family. No matter what challenges life brought them, they trusted that the Lord would provide for every need (Phil 4:19). So the comforting words I leave with you today are: "everything will be all right," not because my mom and grandmother said it (even though they were very convincing), but because the Lord of heaven and earth assures us that it will. Thanks be to God!